# ألف ليلة وليلة

## لطلاب اللغة العربية اللبنانية
(مستوى متوسط)

# One Thousand and One Nights

## for Intermediate Levantine Arabic Language Learners

© 2023 by Matthew Aldrich

The author's moral rights have been asserted. All rights reserved. No part of this document may be reproduced or transmitted in any form or by any means, electronic, mechanical, photocopying, recording, or otherwise, without prior written permission of the publisher.

ISBN: 978-1-949650-97-6

Conceptualized by Matthew Aldrich

Written by Ahmad Al-Masri

Translated (from Egyptian Arabic to Lebanese Arabic) by Charbel Ghaleb

Edited by Matthew Aldrich

Illustrations by Duc-Minh Vu

Audio by Charbel Ghaleb

website: www.lingualism.com

email: contact@lingualism.com

# Table of Contents

II ............................................................. INTRODUCTION

V ................................................... HOW TO USE THIS BOOK

1 ................... الفَصْل الأوّل: المَلِك شَهْريار والوَزير وبِنْتو شَهْرزاد

Chapter 1: King Shahryar, the Vizier,
and his Daughter Scheherazade

11 ................................. الفَصْل الثّاني: قُصِّةْ التّاجِر والجِنّي

Chapter 2: The Tale of the Merchant and the Genie

23 ................................. الفَصْل الثّالِت: الصِياد والسَمْكِة الذَّهبية

Chapter 3: The Fisherman and the Golden Fish

33 ................................. الفَصْل الرّابِع: علاء الدّين والمِصْباح السِّحري

Chapter 4: Aladdin and the Magic Lamp

43 ................................. الفَصْل الخامِس: علي بابا والأَرْبعين حرامي

Chapter 5: Ali Baba and the Forty Thieves

53 ................................. الفَصْل السّادِس: الفِلّاح الذّكي والجِنّي المُشاغِب

Chapter 6: The Clever Farmer and the Mischievous Genie

63 ................................. الفَصْل السّابِع: حرامي إسْكَنْدرية ورئيس الشُّرطة

Chapter 7: The Thief of Alexandria and the Police Chief

73 ................................. الفَصْل التّامِن: العُصْفور الأَزْرق

Chapter 8: The Blue Bird

83 ................................. الفَصْل التّاسِع: البِنْت والسّاحِرة

Chapter 9: The Girl and the Sorceress

93 ................................. الفَصْل العاشِر: الأمير والتِّنين

Chapter 10: The Prince and the Dragon

# Introduction

"**One Thousand and One Nights for Intermediate Levantine Arabic Language Learners**" is a captivating anthology designed specifically for adult Arabic language learners at the intermediate (B1-B2) level. This unique collection features the cherished classic tales in a simplified, yet engaging format, making it an excellent resource for those venturing into the enchanting world of Arabic language and literature.

The book comes with an array of special features to ensure an immersive and effective learning experience:

- **Diacritics for Pronunciation:** We've included diacritical marks (tashkeel) in the Arabic text to assist you in correct pronunciation, and to clarify the meaning of the words, easing your reading experience.

- **Professional Audio Accompaniment:** The book is supplemented with high-quality, slow-paced audio readings by a professional voice artist who is a native Arabic speaker from Egypt. This allows you to listen and mimic the correct pronunciation, intonation, and rhythm of Levantine Arabic.

- **Comprehension Questions and Answers:** Each chapter is followed by a set of comprehension questions, along with their answers. This interactive feature helps to reinforce your understanding of the story and the language constructs used within it.

- **English Translations:** To support your learning, we've provided English translations of the stories. These can be used as a reference to cross-check your understanding of the Arabic text.

All these features work together to provide a comprehensive and enriching learning experience, ensuring you make consistent progress in your Arabic language journey.

The tales in this book have been carefully curated and reimagined to match the language proficiency of intermediate-level learners. We have incorporated level-appropriate vocabulary throughout the stories, ensuring you are neither overwhelmed by complexity nor left unchallenged. To enhance memorization and recognition, we've deliberately woven repetitive patterns of phrases and language structures into the text, encouraging natural language acquisition and recall.

Each chapter is short, and perfectly crafted to be absorbed in a single sitting, allowing you to steadily build your comprehension skills and vocabulary without feeling rushed. The stories retain the intrigue and charm of the original tales, providing you with a sense of accomplishment and enjoyment as you navigate your way through each tale.

As you delve into the enriched narratives found in "One Thousand and One Nights for Intermediate Levantine Arabic Language Learners," you might notice an escalation in language complexity. If at any point the text appears too formidable, we would highly recommend you to revisit "One Thousand and One Nights for Elementary Levantine Arabic Language Learners." The elementary-level book is meticulously designed to provide you with a firm grounding in the most common vocabulary used in the stories and acquaints you with straightforward sentence structures. Spending adequate time with the elementary book can help you grasp the fundamentals of the language effectively. Once you have a solid foundation and feel comfortable with the elementary material, we encourage you to return to the intermediate version. By then, the expanded vocabulary and more advanced sentence structures will no longer seem as daunting but will instead present a rewarding and manageable challenge, fostering your seamless progression towards mastery in Levantine Arabic.

# How to Use This Book

"One Thousand and One Nights for Intermediate Levantine Arabic Language Learners" has been designed to offer flexibility to adapt to your individual learning style. Here's how you can utilize the features of the book according to your needs:

1. **Choose Your Approach:** You have the freedom to approach the stories in multiple ways. You could begin by tackling the Arabic text first, immersing yourself in the structure of the language and the flow of the story. Alternatively, you could start by listening to the accompanying audio, to attune your ear to the sound and rhythm of Levantine Arabic. This can be particularly helpful if you are a more auditory learner.

2. **Use English Translations:** If you're finding the Arabic text or audio challenging, you can refer to the English translations to aid your understanding. Over time, as your comprehension improves, you could challenge yourself by attempting to read or listen to the Arabic without relying on the translations.

3. **Engage with Questions:** You can choose to tackle the comprehension questions before or after reading the story. Attempting them beforehand can provide a

focus for your reading, while answering them after allows you to assess your understanding of the text. Remember, the answers provided in the book are examples and your own answers, while differently worded, may still be correct.

4. **Repetition and Practice:** This book has been designed to promote repetition and practice, key strategies for language learning. We encourage you to revisit chapters and listen to the audio multiple times to reinforce your understanding and memorization.

Remember, the most effective learning strategy is the one that works best for you. So don't be afraid to experiment with different approaches until you find what suits you best.

Visit www.lingualism.com/audio, where you can find the free accompanying audio to download or stream (at variable playback rates).

# الفَصْل الأوّل
## المِلِك شهْرَيار والوَزير وبِنْتو شهْرزاد

كان يا ما كان بِقديم الزّمان، كان في مِلِك إسْمو شهْرَيار بْيُحْكُم ممْلِكِة كْبيرِة وغنية. الملِك شهْرَيار كان بْيِعْتِمد على وَزيرو الأمين الذّكي بإدارِةْ أمور المَمْلِكِة. الوَزير كان عندو بِنْت حِلْوِة وذكية إسْما شهْرزاد، وكانِت مشْهورة بِذكاها النّادِر ومَعْرِفِتا الواسْعة بِالْقُصص والتّاريخ.

بِيَوْم مِن الإيّام، عِرِف المِلك شهْرَيار إنّو مرْتو خانِتو، فا عصّب كْتير وزِعِل. قرّر شهْرَيار إنّو يِتْجوّز كِلّ ليْلِة عروس جْديدِة، ويِقْتِلا تاني يوْم الصُّبِح لما يْكون عنْدا فُرْصة تْخونو. سُلوك المِلك شهْرَيار هَيْدا كان بيخوِّف كِلّ سِتّات وأهالي المَمْلِكِة.

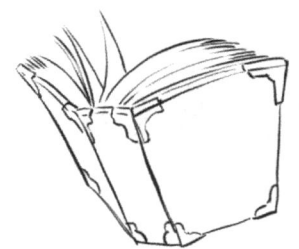

حسّت شهرزاد إنّا لازِم تِتْدخّل لتْخلّص سِتّات المَمْلِكِة وتْرجّع الأمل لشعْبا. قْترحِت على بيّا الوَزير إنّا تِتْجوَّز المِلِك شهْرَيار. ورغْم قلقو وخَوْفو على بِنْتو، وافق الوَزير على طلبا وكان واثِق بِذكاها وحِكْمِتا. قبْل العِرِس، عِمْلِت شهرزاد خُطّة لتِقْنع المِلِك إنّو يبطّل يِقْتُل السِّتّات.

بِليْلِة العِرِس، طلبِت شهرزاد مِن أُخْتا ديناراد تيجي معا عَ قصر المِلِك. ديناراد كانِت عارْفِة خِطّة شهرزاد وعارْفِة إنّو دَوْرا هُوِّ المُساعِدِة والدّعْم. قبْل النّوْم، طلبِت شهرزاد مِن ديناراد تُظْلُب مِنّا تِحْكي قُصّة. بلّشِت شهرزاد تِحْكي قُصّة حِلْوة وشيِّقة لِلْمِلِك شهْرَيار. ووَقِّفِت عَ النُّصّ قبِل ما المِلِك يْنام. كان دوْر ديناراد الأساسي هُوِّ إنّا تْذكّر شهرزاد تْبلِّش القُصّة

وتْبيَّن اِهْتِماما فِيا، وهَيْدا خلّى المِلِك يْحِسّ بِحْشرية ويْحِبّ يِسْمع القُصّة هُوِّ كمان.

تاني يوْم الصُّبِح، كان المِلِك شهْرَيار مِتْشوِّق إنّو يِسْمع باقي القُصّة. قرّر إنّو ما يِقْتُل شهْرزاد وإنّو يَعْطِيا فُرْصة تْكمِّل القُصّة بِاللّيْلة اللي بعْدا. بسّ شهْرزاد عِرْفِت إنّا لازِم تْكون ذكية وتْخلّي كِلّ قُصّة تْطوِّل أكْتر مِن ليْلة وحْدة كِرْمال تِضمن حَياتا.

بِاللّيْلة التّانْية، كمّلِت شهْرزاد القُصّة اللي بلّشِتا، وبلّشِت قُصّة جْديدِة كمان. وبِاللّيالي اللي بعْدا، ضلّت شهْرزاد تِحْكي القُصص الشّيِّقة والمُثيرة اللي فِيا دُروس وعِبر، وهَيْدا خلّى المِلِك شهْرَيار يِنْبِهر بِذكاها وثقافِتا.

كِلّ ليْلة، كانِت دنيازاد بِتِلْعب دوْر مُهِمّ بِتِحْميس الأجْواء وبِداية القُصص. كانِت بِتْضل واعْية وبِتِسْمع شهْرزاد بِاهْتِمام، وهَيْدا كان بيزيد حِشْرية المِلِك وبِيحفْزو يِسْمع كِلّ كِلْمة بِتِتْقال.

بِاللّيْلِة الأولى مِن رِحْلِتا الطّويلة بِالقُصص والحْكايات، بلّشِت شهْرزاد تِحْكي قُصّة لِلمِلك شهْرَيار، قُصّة مِلْيانِة تِشْويق ومُغامرة وحِكْمِة. وهيْك بلّشِت رِحْلِة شهْرزاد الشُّجاعة والحكيمة كِرْمال تْخلِّص سِتّات المَمْلكِة وتِرجِّع الأمن والسّلام لشعْبا.

## Questions

1. شو المِشْكِلة اللي كانِت عِنْد المِلِك شهْرَيار وأثّرِت على سِتّات المَمْلكِة؟

2. شو هِيّ خِطّة شهرزاد كِرْمال تْخلّص سِتّات المَمْلكِة؟

3. كيف ساعِدِت أُخْت شهرزاد، دنيازاد، بِتِنفيذ الخُطّة؟

4. شو قرّر المِلِك شهْرَيار يَعْملو بَعْد ما سِمِع أوّل قُصّة لِشهْرزاد؟

5. شو الهدف مِن إنّو كِلّ قُصّة تْطوّل لِأكْتر مِن ليْلِة وحْدِة؟

# Answers

1. مِشْكِلِةْ المِلِك شهْرَيار كانِت زعلُو بِسبب خِيانِةْ مِرْتو إلو، وقرارو يِتْجوّز وِحْدِة جْدِيدِة كِلّ لِيْلِة ويِقْتِلا تاني يوْم الصُّبِح.

2. خِطّةْ شهْرزاد هِيّ إنّا تِتجوّز المِلِك شهْرَيار وتْخبّرو قُصص مُشوّقة كِلّ لِيْلِة كِرْمال يْبطِّل يِقْتُل السِّتّات.

3. دنيازاد ساعِدِت شهْرزاد مِن وَرا إنّا تْذكِّرا إنّا تْبلِّش القُصّة وتْبيِّن اِهْتِماما فِيا، وهَيْدا خلّى المِلِك يْحِسّ بِحِشْرِيّة ويْحِبّ يِسْمع القُصّة هُوّ كمان.

4. قرّر المِلِك شهْرَيار إنّو ما يِقْتُل شهْرزاد وإنّو يَعْطِيا فُرْصة تْكمِّل القُصّة بِاللّيْلِة اللي بعْدا.

5. الهدف مِن إنّو كِلّ قُصّة تْطوّل لِأكْتر مِن لِيْلِة وِحْدِة هُوّ إنّو شهْرزاد تِضْمن حَياتا ويْكون عِنْدا وَقِت كافي كِرْمال تِقْنِع المِلِك يْبطِّل يِقْتُل السِّتّات.

# Chapter 1: King Shahryar, the Vizier, and his Daughter Scheherazade

In ancient times, a king called Shahryar ruled a vast and rich kingdom. King Shahryar relied on his trustworthy and intelligent vizier to manage the affairs of the kingdom. The vizier had a beautiful and clever daughter named Scheherazade, who was renowned for her exceptional intelligence and wide knowledge of stories and history.

One day, King Shahryar learned of his wife's infidelity, which filled him with great anger and sorrow. He decided to marry a new woman every night and kill her in the morning so that she wouldn't have the chance to betray him. This behavior of King Shahryar caused terror and panic among the women and people of the kingdom.

Scheherazade realized that she must intervene to save the women of the kingdom and restore hope to her people. She proposed to her father, the vizier, that she marry King Shahryar. Despite his concern and fear for his daughter, the vizier agreed to her request due to his trust in her intelligence and wisdom. Before the wedding, Scheherazade devised a plan to convince the king to stop killing the women.

On her wedding night, Scheherazade asked her sister, Dinarzad, to come with her to the palace of the king. Dinarzad knew of Scheherazade's plan and understood that her role was to assist and support her. Before sleep,

Scheherazade asked Dinarzad to request a story from her. Scheherazade began telling a fascinating and interesting story to King Shahryar and stopped in the middle before the king fell asleep. Dinarzad's main role was to remind Scheherazade to start the story and show interest in listening, which made the king curious and eager to hear the story as well.

The next morning, King Shahryar longed to hear the rest of the story. He decided not to kill Scheherazade and gave her a chance to finish the story the next night. But Scheherazade knew that she must be wise and make each story last more than one night to ensure her life.

On the second night, Scheherazade finished the story she began and started a new one. Over the following nights, Scheherazade continued telling thrilling and captivating stories that contained wisdom and morals, which astonished King Shahryar with her intelligence and culture.

Every night, Dinarzad played a vital role in enlivening the atmosphere and starting the stories. She remained awake and listened attentively to Scheherazade, which aroused the king's curiosity and motivated him to listen to every word uttered.

On the first night of this long journey of tales and stories, Scheherazade began telling a story to King Shahryar, a story full of excitement, adventure, and wisdom. And so began the brave and wise journey of Scheherazade to save the women of the kingdom and restore safety and peace to her people.

Questions

1. What was King Shahryar's problem that affected the women of the kingdom?
2. What was Scheherazade's plan to save the women of the kingdom?
3. How did Scheherazade's sister, Dinarzad, help execute the plan?
4. What did King Shahryar decide after hearing Scheherazade's first story?
5. What was the goal of making each story last more than one night?

Answers

1. King Shahryar's problem was his anger over his wife's infidelity and his decision to marry a new woman every night and kill her in the morning.
2. Scheherazade's plan was to marry King Shahryar and tell him thrilling and captivating stories every night to make him stop killing women.
3. Dinarzad helped Scheherazade by reminding her to start the story and show interest in listening, which made the king curious and eager to hear the story as well.

4. King Shahryar decided not to kill Scheherazade and gave her a chance to finish the story the next night.

5. The goal of making each story last more than one night was to ensure Scheherazade's life and give her enough time to convince the king to stop killing women.

# الفَصْل التّاني
# قُصِّةُ التّاجِر والجِنّي

بِاللّيلِة التّانْية مِن قُصص شهرزاد، بلّشِت بِقُصّة عن تاجِر غني وجِنّي قَوي كْتير. بِيوْم مِن الإيّام، قرّر التّاجِر إنّو يْسافِر لمدينِة بْعيدِة كِرْمال يْبيع بْضاعْتو. قِبل ما يْبلِّش رِحِلْتو، وِقِف بِغابِة هادْيِة كِرْمال يِرْتاح شْوَيّ وياكُل.

بالْغابِة، كسر التّاجِر غُصِن شجرة كِرْمال يْوَلِّع نار لَيْسخِّن فيا

أكُلو. بسّ فجْأة، ظهر جِنّي قَوي ومْعصّب كْتير قِدّام التّاجِر وصرخ وقلّو: "يا زلمي إنْتَ، إنْتَ كسرْت غُصْن الشجرة اللي أنا كِنْت ساكِن فِيا، كِرْمال هيْك حاقِتْلك!"

نِقز التّاجِر ونْرعب، وبلّش يِتْحايَل على الجِنّي ليْسامْحو ويِتْركو يْعيش. قال لْلْجِنّي إنّو عنْدو عيْلة وأصحاب مِعْتِمدين عليْه وإنّن حَيْموتوا مِن الزّعل لوْ مات. سِمع الجِنّي التّاجِر وقرّر إنّو يَعْطي فُرصة ليْكفّر عن غلْطِتو.

وَعد الجِنّي التّاجِر إنّو حَيِسْمحلو يِرْجع لعيلْتو لِمِدّة سِنة وِحْدة كِرْمال يْوَدِّعُن ويْسدّد دْيونو، بسّ بِشرْط إنّو يِرْجع بعْد ما تُخْلص السّنِة هَيْدي كِرْمال يِقِتْلو. وافق التّاجِر على الشّرْط ورِجع لِمدينْتو وقلْبو مِلْيان زعل وخوْف.

و لمّا خِلْصِت السّنِة، بلّش التّاجِر رِحْلِة الرّجْعة لِلْغابة كِرْمال يْواجِه مصيرو اللي كان مكْتِبلو. وعَ الطّريق، قابل زلمي خِتْيار ماسِك عصايِة طَويلة. صار التّاجِر يْخبّرو قِصّتو مع الجِنّي وعن الوَعْد اللي وَعدو فيه. شِفِق الخِتْيار على التّاجِر وقرّر إنّو يِمْشي معو لِلْغابة.

و هِنَّ بِرِحْلِتُن، قابِل التّاجِر والخِتْيار رِجّالَين تانْيين: واحِد حامِل جرِّةْ مايْ والتّانِي معو حبِل طَويل. نْضمّ الرِّجّالَين للتّاجِر والرِّجّال الخِتْيار وراحوا كُلُّن عَ الْغابِة كِرْمال يْواجْهوا الجِنّي.

لمّا وِصلوا عَ الغابِة، ظهر الجِنّي وهدّد إنّو يِقْتُل التّاجِر. تْدخّل الرِّجّال الخِتْيار وسأل الجِنّي اِذا بْيِسمحْلو يِسألوا تْلات أسْئِلة قبِل ما يِقْتُل التّاجِر. وافق الجِنّي على طلب الرِّجّال الخِتْيار.

سأل الخِتْيار السُّؤال الأوّل عن حالو: "لَيْش العصايِة الطَّويلِة هَيْدي مُفيدِة إلي؟" وجَوابو إنّو كان بْيِسْتعْمِلا كِرْمال يْقيس عُمْق النّهر قبِل ما يِقْطعو لَيِضمن سلامْتو. وبعْدَين سأل الخِتْيار السُّؤال التّاني: "شو فايْدِةْ الجرّة؟" فا ردّ الرِّجّال اللي كان شايِل الجرّة إنّو بْيِسْتعْمِلا يْشيل فِيا الماي ويِقدر يْطفّي فِيا النّار لَوْ صار حريقة. أخيراً، سأل الخِتْيار السُّؤال التّالِت: "لَيْش حامِل معك الحبْل الطَّويل هَيْدا؟" فا ردّ الرِّجّال التّالِت إنّو بْيِسْتعْمِل الحبِل كِرْمال يِتْسلّق في الجْبال تَيِقدر يْخلّص حَياةْ النّاس اللي محجوزين عَ العالي.

و بِناءً على رُدود الأسْئِلة التَّلاتِة، قال الخِتْيار لِلْجِنّي: "الرِّجّال هوْل سْتَعْمَلوا الأدَوات هَيْدي كِرْمال يْساعْدوا ويخَلِّصوا النّاس، وهَيْدا بيعَلِّمْنا إنّو الحَياةْ قيِّمة ولازِم نَعْمُل اللي مْنِقدر عليه كِرْمال نْعيش بِسلام وتعاوُن. هَيْدا ما بيعَلِّمك شي يا جِنّي؟" تأثَّر الجِنّي بِحكي الخِتْيار وقرَّر يِتْرُك التّاجِر يعيش ويِعْفي عنّو.

بعْد التَّجْرِبة المُرعْبِة الصَّعبِة هَيْدي، رِجع التّاجِر لمدينْتو وشكر الرِّجال التَّلاتِة على مُساعْدِتُن وتضحِيِّتُن. ورُغْم الخوْف والتَّوَتُّر اللي كان حاسِس فِيُن، إلّا إنّو التّاجِر تعلّم قيمِة التَّعاوُن والصَّداقة وعِرِف إنّو الحَياةْ بِتْعَلِّمْنا دُروس وعِبر كْتيرة.

بِالوَقِت هَيْدا، كان المِلِك شهْرَيار عم بْيِسمع قُصَّة شهْرزاد بِاهْتِمام كْتير. صار يِتعلّق بْشخْصِيّات القُصّة ويِتعاطف مع مشاعِرُن ومعاناتُن. وبِفضل القُصّة هَيْدي، بلَّش المِلِك يْشوف الحَياة بِنظرة جْديدِة ويَعْرِف إنّو النّاس مُمْكِن يِتْغيَّروا وإنّو بِناخُد الحِكْمة والعِبر مِن التَّجارُب المُخْتِلفة.

بِاللَّيلِة اللي بَعْدا، خَلِّصت شهْرزاد قُصِّة التّاجِر والجِنّي وبلَّشِت تِحْكي قُصّة جْديدِة. وعلى هَيْدا الحال، ضلّت شهْرزاد تْقوّي

الثِّقة بَيْنّا وبيْن المَلِك شهْرَيار، وعلّمِتو دُروس قيِّمة عن الحُبّ والإنْسانية والعَدِل مِن وَرا القُصص الرّائعة اللي ملْيانِة حِكم.

و مع كِلّ قُصّة شهْرزاد بِتْخبِّرا، كانِت دينازاد معا وبِتْساعِدا لتْخلّي المَلِك مِهتمّ ومُتشوِّق إنّو يِسْمع كمان وكمان. وبِالطّريقة هَيْدي، كانِت شهْرزاد عم بِتْخلِّص حالا هِيّ وكِلّ سِتّات المَمْلِكِة يوْم بعْد يوْم، وكانِت بِتْساعِد المَلِك شهْرَيار إنّو يِفْهم ويِتْغيّر عن جدّ.

## Questions

1. ليْش الجِنّي ظهر عَ التّاجِر وهدّد إنّو يِقِتْلو؟

2. شو الشّرْط اللي حطّو الجِنّي للتّاجِر قبِل ما يِقِتْلو؟

3. مين النّاس اللي قابِلُن التّاجِر هُوّ ورايِح يواجِهْ الجِنّي؟

4. كيف الرِّجّال الخِتْيار قِدِر يِقْنِع الجِنّي إنّو ما يِقْتُل التّاجِر؟

5. شو العِبْرة اللي تْعلّما التّاجِر مِن القُصّة هَيْدي؟

## Answers

1. ظهر الجِنّي عَ التّاجِر وهدّد إنّو يِقْتْلو كِرْمال التّاجِر كسر غُصْن الشّجرة اللي هُوِّ ساكِن فِيا.

2. الشّرْط اللي حطّو الجِنّي هُوِّ إنّو يِسمح للتّاجِر يِرْجع لَعيلْتو لمُدّة سِنة كِرْمال يْوَدِّعُن ويْسدِّد دْيونو، بسّ لازِم يِرْجع بعْد ما تُخْلص السِّنة لَيِقْتْلو.

3. قابل التّاجِر زلمي خِتْيار ماسِك عصايِة طَويلة، وزلمي شايِل جرّة ماي، وواحد تاني معو حبِل طَويل.

4. قِدِر الرِّجّال الخِتْيار يِقْنِع الجِنّي إنّو ما بِقْتُل التّاجِر عن طريق إنّو يْفرّجي قيمةْ الحَياةْ وكيف مُمْكِن نِسْتعْمِل أدْوات مِخْتِلْفِة كِرْمال نْعيش بِسلام وتعاوُن.

5. التّاجِر تْعلّم مِن القُصّة هَيْدي قيمةْ التّعاوُن والصّداقة وعِرِف إنّو الحَياةْ بِتْعلِّمْنا دُروس وعِبر كْتيرِة.

## Chapter 2: The Tale of the Merchant and the Genie

On the second night of Scheherazade's stories, she began narrating a tale about a wealthy merchant and a powerful genie. One day, the merchant decided to travel to a faraway city to sell his goods. Before starting his journey, he stopped at a peaceful forest to rest and have his meal.

In the forest, the merchant cut a branch of a tree to light a fire and warm his food. Suddenly, a furious and powerful genie appeared before the merchant and yelled, "Oh human, you have cut the branch of the tree that was my shelter, and for that, I will kill you!"

The merchant was frightened and panicked, and he began pleading with the genie to forgive him and spare his life. He told the genie that he had a family and friends who relied on him, and they would die of grief if they lost him. The genie listened to the merchant and decided to give him a chance to make amends for his mistake.

The genie promised the merchant that he would allow him to return to his family for a period of one year to say goodbye to them and pay off his debts, but on the condition that he would return after the year had passed for the genie to kill him. The merchant agreed to the condition and returned to his city with a heavy heart filled with sadness and fear.

At the end of the year, the merchant started his journey back to the forest to face his inevitable fate. On the way, he met an old man carrying a long stick. The merchant narrated his story to the old man about the genie and the promise he made. The old man showed sympathy to the merchant and decided to accompany him to the forest.

As they continued their journey, the merchant and the old man met two other men: one carrying a jug of water and the other holding a long rope. The two men joined the merchant and the old man, and they all headed toward the forest to confront the genie.

When they reached the forest, the genie appeared and threatened to kill the merchant. The old man intervened and asked the genie if he would allow him to ask three questions before he killed the merchant. The genie agreed to the old man's request.

The old man asked the first question about himself, "How did the long stick benefit me?" and he answered that he used it to measure the depth of the river before crossing it to ensure his safety. Then the old man asked the second question, "What is the benefit of the jug?" and the man carrying the jug replied that he used it to store water and could use it to extinguish a fire in case of an emergency. Finally, the old man asked the third question, "Why are you carrying the long rope?" and the third man replied that he used the rope to climb mountains and could use it to save people stranded on its peaks.

Based on the answers of the three questions, the old man told the genie, "The three of us used these tools for help and survival, and this teaches us that life is valuable, and we must use what is in our hands to live in peace and cooperation. Didn't you consider that, O genie?" The genie was moved by the old man's words and decided to spare the merchant and forgive him.

After this terrifying and difficult experience, the merchant returned to his city and thanked the three men for their help and sacrifice. Despite his fear and the tension he went through, the merchant learned the value of cooperation and friendship and that life carries many lessons and wisdom.

Meanwhile, King Shahryar listened passionately to the story of Scheherazade. He began to develop an attachment to the characters of the story and sympathize with their feelings and struggles. Thanks to this story, the king began to see life through new eyes and realized that people could change and that wisdom and lessons come from different experiences.

On the following night, Scheherazade finished telling the story of the merchant and the genie and began to narrate a new story. In this way, Scheherazade continued to establish trust between her and King Shahryar and taught him valuable lessons about love, humanity, and justice through wonderful stories full of wisdom.

With each story told by Scheherazade, Dinarzad was always by her side, playing her role in making the king interested and eager to hear more. Thus, Scheherazade saved herself and the women of the kingdom day by day while leading King Shahryar toward true understanding and change.

Questions

1. Why did the genie appear to the merchant and threaten to kill him?
2. What was the condition that the genie set for the merchant before killing him?
3. Who were the people that the merchant met on his journey to confront the genie?
4. How did the old man manage to convince the genie not to kill the merchant?
5. What lesson did the merchant learn from this experience?

Answers

1. The genie appeared to the merchant and threatened to kill him because the merchant cut a branch from the tree, which was the genie's shelter.
2. The condition that the genie set for the merchant before killing him was to allow him to return to his

family for one year to say goodbye to them and collect his debts, but he must return after the year to be killed.

3. The merchant met an old man carrying a long stick, a man carrying a jar of water, and another holding a long rope.

4. The old man managed to convince the genie not to kill the merchant by showing the value of life and how different tools can be used to live in peace and cooperation.

5. The merchant learned from this experience the value of cooperation and friendship and that life holds many lessons and wisdom.

# الفَصْل التّالِت
# الصِيّاد والسَّمْكِة الذَّهبية

بِمَمْلِكِة بْعيدِة، كان في صِيّاد فقير عايِش مع مرْتو بِكوخ صْغير على البحِر. كان بْيِتصيّد لَيِصرُف على عيْلتو الصْغيرِة. بِيوْم مِن الإيّام، كبّ الصَّيّاد شبكْتو بِالبحِر لِيتصيّد سمك لَيْبيعو بِالسّوق. بعْد ما نطر ساعات طَويلة، لمّ الشّبكِة ولِقي فيا سمْكِة ذهبية صْغيرِة محْبوسِة بيْن الحْبال.

تْفاجِئ الصِيّاد بِالاِكْتِشاف هَيْدا. وتْطلّع بِالسَّمْكِة الذّهبية اللي كانِت بْتِلمع بِألْوان حِلْوِة عَ نور الشِّمس. فجْأة، بلّشِت السَّمْكِة تِحكي بِصوْت واضِح، وطلبِت مِن الصِيّاد يِتْرِكا تعيش وهِيِّ حتْحقِّقْلُو تلات أُمْنِيّات.

فكّر الصِيّاد بِالعرْض المُغْري هَيْدا، وبعْد ترَدُّد، قرّر إنّو يْوافِق على طلب السَّمْكِة الذّهبية. وبعْد ما الصِيّاد ترَكا، طلب أُمْنِيّتو الأولى: بيْت جْديد ومُريح لعيْلْتو. فا ظهر بيْت فخِم حدّ الكوخ القديم صُغري.

الصِيّاد ومرْتو ما صدّقوا قدّيْش محْظوظين، وشكروا السَّمْكِة الذّهبية وعاشوا حَياةْ مِرتاحة بِبيْتُن الجْديد. بعْد مِدّة، قرّر الصِيّاد يروح مرّة تانْيِة عَ البجر لَيُطْلُب أُمْنِيّتو التّانْيِة: إنّو يصير غني ويِتْمتّع بِثرْوِة كْبيرِة. وبِاللّحْظة اللي تْمنّى فيا هيْك، مْتلِت خِزْنِةْ بَيْتو بِالدَّهب والجَواهِر.

بِالثَّرْوِة الكْبيرِة هَيْدي، صار الصِيّاد ومرْتو مِن أغْنى النّاس بِالْممْلكِة. شْتروا تْياب فخْمِة وعِمْلوا عزايم عشا لأصْحابُن وجيرانُن، وعاشوا حَياةْ الأغْنِيا. ومع هيْدا، بلّش الصِيّاد يْحِسّ بِالْفراغ، وإنّو بِدّو شغْلات أكْتر مِن هيْك، فا قرّر يُطْلُب أُمْنِيّتو

التّالِتة مِن السّمْكِة الذّهبية.

راح الصِيّاد عَ الشّطّ وعيّط لالسّمْكِة الذّهبية، اللي طِلْعِت مِن الماي وسِمْعِت طلبو. قال الصِيّاد: "بدّي صير مِلِك على المَمْلِكِة هَيْدي وأُحْكُما بِعدِل ورحْمة." وافقِت السّمْكِة الذّهبية على طلبو وتْحقّقِت أُمْنِيّتو صُغْري.

الصِيّاد صار مِلِك عظيم وعاش بِقصر رائِع مع مرْتو وأُمراؤو. حكم بِعدِل ورحْمة وحاوِل يْحسّن حَياةْ شعْبو. بسّ مع مُرور الوَقِت، بلّش يْعاني مِن القلق والضُّغوط اللي بْتيجي مع الحُكِم، وحسّ بِالتّعب والغضب مِن التّحدِّيّات اليَوْمية.

و بِلِيْلية هادْية، فكّر المِلِك الصِيّاد بِحَياتو وتْذكّر الإيّام البسيطة لمّا كان يِتْصيّد سمك وعايِش بِسلام مع مرْتو. قلْبو وَجعو لمّا تْذكّر إنّو الإيّام هَيْدي راحِت، وقرّر إنّو يُطْلُب مُساعِدِةْ السّمْكِة الذّهبية مرّة تانْية.

راح المِلِك عَ الشَّطّ وعيّط للسّمْكِة، اللي طلعِت مِن الماي. طلب مِنّا تُرجْعو لحَياتو البسيطة اللي كان فِيا صيّاد فقير، وتاخُد معا كِلّ الثّروات والمُلْك. بْتسِمِت السّمْكِة الذّهبية

ووافِقِت على طلبو، فا رِجِع الصِيّاد ومرْتو عَ الكوخ البسيطْ على الشّطّ وعاشوا حَياةْ هادْية وسعيدِة ملْيانِة بِالْمحبّة والرِّضا.

كِل الوَقِت هَيْدا، كان المِلِك شهْرَيار عم بْيِسْمع قُصّةْ شهْرزاد بِدهْشِة واهْتِمام. صار يِتْعلّق بِشخْصِيّةْ الصِيّاد ويِتْعجّب مِن حِكْمةْ السّمْكِة الذّهبية. بعْد ما شهْرزاد خلّصِت قِصّتا، قال المِلِك شهْرَيار إنّو بدّو يِسْمع قُصص أكْتر وإنّو مِش حَيقْتِلا تاني يوْم الصُّبِح.

## Questions

1. شو لاقا الصِيّاد بِشبِكْتو لمّا شالا مِن البحِر؟

2. شو اللي عرضِتو السّمْكِة الذّهبية على الصِيّاد مُقابِل تحْريرا؟

3. شو الأُمْنية التّانْية اللي طلبا الصِيّاد مِن السّمْكِة الذّهبية؟

4. شو كان شُعور المِلِك الصِيّاد بعْد ما صار مِلِك على المَمْلِكِة؟

5. شو الطّلب الأخير اللي طلبو المِلِك الصِيّاد مِن السّمْكِة الذّهبية؟

## Answers

1. لِقي الصِيّاد سمْكِة ذهبية صْغيرِة محبوسِة بيْن الحْبال.

2. عرضِت السّمْكِة الذّهبية تحْقيق تْلات أُمْنِيّات لِلصِيّاد مُقابِل إنّو يِتْرِكا تْعيش.

3. طلب الصِيّاد إنّو يْصير غني ويِتْمتّع بِثرْوِة كْبيرِة.

4. بلّش المَلِك الصِيّاد يْعاني مِن القلق والضُّغوط اللي بْتيجي مع الحُكْم، وحسّ بِالتّعب والغضب مِن التّحدِّيّات اليَوْمية.

5. طلب المَلِك الصِيّاد إنّو يِرْجع تاني لَحَياتو البسيطة اللي كان فِيا صِيّاد فقير، وتاخُد السّمْكِة الذّهبية معا كِلّ الثّروات والمُلْك.

# Chapter 3: The Fisherman and the Golden Fish

In a distant kingdom, there was a poor fisherman who lived with his wife in a small hut by the sea. He relied on fishing to support his small family. One day, the fisherman cast his net into the sea in search of fish to sell in the market. After hours of waiting, he pulled up his net and found a small golden fish trapped among the ropes.

The fisherman was surprised by this discovery and marveled at the golden fish that shimmered in bright colors under the sunlight. Suddenly, the fish began to speak in a clear voice and asked the fisherman to spare its life in exchange for granting him three wishes.

The fisherman thought about this tempting offer and, after some hesitation, decided to agree to the golden fish's request. And when he released it, the fisherman made his first wish: a new and comfortable home for his family. A luxurious house appeared next to the old hut immediately.

The fisherman and his wife could not believe their good luck and thanked the golden fish. They lived a luxurious life in their new home. After some time, the fisherman wanted to go to the sea again to make his second wish: to become rich and have immense wealth. And at the moment he wished for it, his house was filled with gold and jewels.

With this immense wealth, the fisherman and his wife became some of the richest people in the kingdom. They bought luxurious clothes and held dinner parties for their friends and neighbors, and lived the life of nobles. However, the fisherman began to feel empty and wanted more, so he decided to make his third wish to the golden fish.

The fisherman went to the beach and called out to the golden fish that emerged from the water and listened to his request. The fisherman said, "I want to become the king of this kingdom and rule it with justice and mercy." The golden fish agreed to his request, and his wish was immediately granted.

The fisherman became a great king and lived in a magnificent palace with his wife and princes. He ruled with justice and mercy and sought to improve the lives of his people. But over time, he began to suffer from the increasing pressure and anxiety that comes with ruling, and felt tired and angry from the daily challenges.

On a quiet night, the fisherman king reflected on his life and remembered the simple days when he used to fish and live in peace with his wife. His heart ached for those days, and he decided to seek the help of the golden fish once again.

The king went to the beach and called out to the golden fish that emerged from the water. He asked her to return him to his simple life as a poor fisherman and to take all of his wealth and possessions with it. The golden fish smiled and granted his request, so the fisherman and his wife returned to their simple hut on the beach and lived a quiet and happy life filled with love and contentment.

Meanwhile, King Shahryar listened to Scheherazade's story with amazement and interest. He began to relate to the fisherman's character and admired the wisdom of the golden fish. After Scheherazade finished her story, King Shahryar announced that he wanted to hear more stories and that he would not kill her the next morning.

Questions

1. What did the fisherman find in his net when he pulled it out of the sea?
2. What did the golden fish offer the fisherman in exchange for its release?
3. What was the second wish that the fisherman asked the golden fish to grant him?
4. How did the king fisherman feel after becoming the ruler of the kingdom?
5. What was the last request that king the fisherman made to the golden fish?

Answers

1. The fisherman found a small golden fish trapped in the ropes.

2. The golden fish offered to grant three wishes to the fisherman in exchange for sparing its life.

3. The fisherman asked to become rich and enjoy immense wealth.

4. The king fisherman felt anxious and overwhelmed with the pressures that come with ruling, tired and angry with the daily challenges.

5. King fisherman asked to return to his simple life as a poor fisherman and for the golden fish to take all the wealth and the kingdom.

# الفَصْل الرّابِع
## علاء الدّين والمِصْباح السِّحْري

بِاللّيلةِ اللي بعْدا، بلّشِت شهْرزاد تِحْكي لِلْملِك شهْرَيار قُصّة ملْيانةِ تفاصيل مُشوّقة عن علاء الدّين والمصباح السّحري.

علاء الدّين كان شبّ فقير عايِش مع إمّو الأرْملِة بِحيّ مِن أحْيا المدينةِ. كان بْيِشْتِغِل الصُّبِح وبِيِتْمشّى بِالأسْواق والشَّوارع، وكانِت إمّو بْتَعْمُل شِغْل البيْت.

بِيوْم مِن الإيّام، وعلاء الدّين بْيِتمشّى بِالسّوق، قابل زلمي غريب قلّو إنّو عمّو اللي كانِت إمّو بْتِحكي عنّو. الرّجّال الغريب قلّو إنّو جاي لَيْزور عيْلْتو، وإنّو عارِف محل سِرّي في كنْز كْبير مخبّى. الكنْز هَيْدا مُمْكِن يْصير مِفْتاح الغِنى والنّجاح لعلاء الدّين وإمّو. ورغْم شُكوك علاء الدين، إلّا إنّو قرّر يْروح مع الرّجّال الغريب يْنبِّش على الكنْز.

الرّجّال الغريب وَصلُو لمُغارة مِعتِمة ومْخبّاية بِالصّحرا. طلب مِن علاء الدّين يْفوت عَ المغارة ويْجيب المِصباح القديم اللي فيا، وقلّو إنّو المِصباح هَيْدا في قُوّة سِحرية مِش مُمْكِن يِتْخيّلا. فات علاء الدّين المُغارة ولِقي المِصباح السِّحري. بسّ بِمُجرّد ما مِسكو، قفل الرّجّال الغريب باب المُغارة وترك علاء الدّين محْبوس جُوّا، وكان ناوي إنّو بِسْرُق المِصباح مِنّو بعْديْن.

بِمُحاوْلة لَيُضْهر مِن المُغارة، صار علاء الدّين يْنبِّش على طريق الخُروج. لِقي المِصباح القديم وفكّر إنّو مُمْكِن يْضوّي في المْغارة المْعتِمة ويْنبِّش على المخرْج. مسك المِصباح

السِّحْري وفجْأة ظهر جِنّي كْبير. قلّو الجِنّي: "أنا جِنّي المِصباح السِّحْري، وأنا هون كِرْمال حقّقْلك تْلات أُمْنيّات تْطْلُبا." علاء الدِّين ما كان فاهم شو عم بْيصير، بسّ قرّر إنّو يِسْتغِلّ الفُرْصة كِرْمال يِطْلع مِن المْغارة. طلب مِن الجِنّي ياخدو عبّيتو بِالْمدينة، وبِثانْيَة وِحْدِة لِقي علاء الدِّين حالو حدّ إمّو اللي كانِت قِلْقانِة عليْه وما كانِت عارْفِة شو صرْلو. علاء الدِّين قال لإِمّوعن الجِنّي والمِصباح السِّحْري. صاروا يِفْهموا قُوَّة المِصباح وكيف يِقْدْروا يِسْتعِمْلوه كِرْمال يْحسّنوا حَياتُن.

طلب علاء الدِّين مِن الجِنّي يْجيبْلُن ثرْوِة كْبيرِة تْخلّيُن يعيشوا بِرفاهية. ومِن وَرا الثّرْوِة هَيْدي، تْغيّرِت حَياةْ علاء الدِّين وإمّو كِلّياً. شْتروا قصِر حِلو وصار علاء الدِّين شخْصية مُهِمّة بِالْمدينة. مع الوَقِت، حسّ علاء الدِّين إنّو بدّو يِتْجوّز الأميرة الجِلْوِة، بِنْت السُّلْطان. سْتعْمل المِصباح السِّحْري كِرْمال يْساعْدو يِرْبح قلْب الأميرة ويِتْجوّزا.

بِهَيْدا الوَقِت، رجِع الرّجّال الغريب كِرْمال يُرجِّع المِصْباح السِّحْري اللي كان مْفكِّروا إنّو نْسرق مِنّو. كان بدّو يِسْرقو مِن علاء الدِّين ويِسْتعْمِل قُوُّنو كِرْمال يِتْحكّم بِالْمدينة ويِفْرُض

سَيْطرْتو على سِكّانا. بسّ علاء الدّين والأميرة تْعاونوا مع بعْض كِرْمال يِقاوْموا الخطر اللي كان عم بيهدِّد حَياتُن ومُسْتقْبل المدينة.

بِالْمعْركة الأخيرة، قِدِر علاء الدّين والأميرة يْرجِّعوا المِصْباح السّحْري مِن الرِّجّال الغريب ويْخسْروه. حْتفظ علاء الدّين بِالمِصْباح، بسّ قرّر إنّو مِش حَيتِّكِل عليْه بِالمُستقْبل إلّا بِالْحالات الضّروريّة كْتير. تْجوّز علاء الدّين الأميرة وعاشوا مبْسوطين عَ طول.

لمّا خلّصِت شهْرزاد قُصّة علاء الدّين والمِصْباح السّحْري، كان المِلِك شهْرَيار مُنْبهِر بِالْقُصّة، ومِتْشوّق إنّو يِسْمع القُصص تانْية مُلْهِمة ومُثيرِة. فِهِم المِلِك شهْرَيار إنّو كِلّ قُصّة فيا دُروس مُهِمّة عن الحَياةْ والحِكْمِة والعدِل.

## Questions

1. كيف علاء الدّين قابل الرّجّال الغريب؟

2. شو اللي طلبو الرّجّال الغريب مِن علاء الدّين لمّا أخدو عَ المُغارة؟

3. كيف علاء الدّين قِدِر يهْرُب مِن المغارة؟

4. كيف علاء الدّين سْتعْمل المِصْباح السّحْري كِرمال يْحسِّن حَياتو هُوّ وإمّو؟

5. شو الخطر اللي علاء الدّين والأميرة واجهوه؟

# Answers

1. علاء الدّين قابل الرِّجّال الغريب هُوّ وعم بيتْمشّى بِالسّوق.

2. طلب مِن علاء الدّين يْفوت عَ المْغارة ويجيب المِصْباح القديم اللي هونيك.

3. قِدِر علاء الدّين يِهرُب مِن المغارة بِمُساعْدِة الجِنّي اللي طِلِع لمّا فرك المِصْباح السِّحْري.

4. طلب علاء الدّين مِن الجِنّي يجيبْلُن ثرْوِة كْبيرِة، وهَيْدا سمحْلُن يِشْتِروا قصْر حِلو ويغيّروا حَياتُن كِلِّيًا.

5. الزّلمي الغريب رِجع كِرْمال ياخُد المِصْباح السِّحْري ويِسْتعْمِل قُوتو كِرْمال يِتْحكّم بِالْمدينة، بسّ علاء الدّين والأميرة وِقْفوا بْوِجّوا وخسّروه بِالْمعْركِة الأخيرة.

## Chapter 4: Aladdin and the Magic Lamp

On the following night, Scheherazade began to tell an intricate and captivating story about Aladdin and the Magic Lamp to King Shahryar.

Aladdin was a poor young man who lived with his widowed mother in one of the city's neighborhoods. He worked during the day, wandering through the markets and streets, while his mother did household chores.

One day, while Aladdin was strolling through the market, he met a strange man who claimed to be his long-lost uncle, whom Aladdin had only heard about from his mother. The stranger claimed that he had come to visit his family and that he knew of a secret place where a great treasure was hidden. This treasure could be the key to Aladdin's and his mother's wealth and success. Despite his suspicions, Aladdin decided to join the strange man on a quest to find the treasure.

The man led him to a dark and secret cave in the depths of the desert. He asked Aladdin to enter the cave and retrieve the old lamp that was there, indicating that this lamp possessed an unimaginable magical power. Aladdin sneaked into the cave and found the magic lamp. However, once he held it, the stranger closed the cave's entrance and left Aladdin trapped inside, planning to steal the lamp from him later.

In an attempt to get out of the cave, Aladdin started looking for a way out. He found the old lamp and thought it might be useful to light up the dark cave and to search for the exit. He began to rub the magic lamp, and suddenly a giant genie appeared. The genie told him, "I am the genie of the magic lamp, and I am here to grant three wishes that you asked for." Aladdin did not fully comprehend what was happening, but he decided to seize the opportunity to escape from the cave. He asked the genie to transport him to his home in the city, and in the blink of an eye, Aladdin found himself next to his mother, who had been worried about her son's fate. Aladdin told his mother what had happened and about the genie and the magic lamp. They both began to realize the lamp's power and how it could be used to improve their lives.

Aladdin asked the genie to bring them immense wealth that would allow them to live in luxury. Thanks to this wealth, Aladdin's and his mother's lives changed completely. They bought a beautiful palace, and Aladdin became an important figure in the city. As time passed, Aladdin realized that he wanted to marry the beautiful princess, the sultan's daughter. He used the magic lamp to help him win the princess's heart and allow him to marry her.

In the meantime, the strange man returned to reclaim the magic lamp that he felt was stolen from him. He planned to steal it from Aladdin and use its power to control the city and impose his dominance over its inhabitants. But Aladdin and the princess cooperated to confront the danger threatening their lives and the future of the city.

In the final battle, Aladdin and the princess managed to retrieve the magic lamp from the strange man and defeat him. Aladdin kept the lamp but pledged not to rely on it in the future except in cases of extreme necessity. Aladdin and the princess got married and lived happily ever after.

Scheherazade finished telling the story of Aladdin and the magic lamp to King Shahriyar. The king was fascinated by this story and eager to hear more inspiring and exciting tales. King Shahriyar realized that every story carries important lessons about life, wisdom, and justice.

Questions

1. How did Aladdin meet the mysterious man?
2. What did the mysterious man ask Aladdin to do when he took him to the cave?
3. How did Aladdin escape from the cave?
4. How did Aladdin use the magic lamp to improve his and his mother's life?
5. What danger did Aladdin and the princess face?

Answers

1. Aladdin met the mysterious man when he was wandering in the market.

2. The mysterious man asked Aladdin to enter the cave and bring the old lamp that was there.

3. Aladdin managed to escape from the cave by requesting help from the genie who came out when he rubbed the magic lamp.

4. Aladdin asked the genie to bring them immense wealth, which allowed them to buy a beautiful palace and completely change their lives.

5. The mysterious man returned to retrieve the magic lamp and use its power to control the city, but Aladdin and the princess confronted him and defeated him in the final battle.

# الفَصْل الخامِس
# علي بابا والأرْبعين حرامي

لمّا خلّصِت شهْرزاد قُصّةْ علاء الدّين والمِصْباح السّحْري، كان المَلِك شهْرَيار ناطِر بِفارِغ الصّبِر يِسْمع قُصص تانْية عجيبة وملْيانِة مُغامرات. وبِاللّيْلِة هَيْدي، بلّشِت شهْرزاد تْخبّرو قُصّةْ علي بابا والأرْبعين حرامي.

علي بابا كان زلمي بسيط وفقير، كان ساكِن بِضيْعة بْعيدِة مع

مرْتو وإبْنو. وبيوْم مِن الإيّام، كان علي بابا عم بِلِمّ الحطب بِالغابِة لمّا سِمع صوْت حَوافِر على الأرْض وزْجال عم يِحْكوا بِصوْت عالي. فجأةُ ظهر قِدّامو زلمي شكْلُو زعيم عِصابِة مِألِّفة مِن أرْبعين حرامي، ولمّا وِصلوا عَ صخْرة كْبيرِة، قال الزّعيم كِلْمةْ سِرّ: "اِفْتح يا سِمْسِيم!" وفِعْلاً فتِحت الصّخْرة وظهر مدْخل سِرّي لمْغارة كْبيرِة مِلْيانِة كْنوز ودهب.

بعْد ما الحرامية فلّوا مِن المْغارة، راح علي بابا عَ الصّخْرة العِمْلاقة وسْتعْمل كِلْمةْ السّرّ كِرْمال يِفْتح المدْخل. ولمّا فات عَ المْغارة، تْفاجأ بِكمِّيّةْ الكْنوزالكْبيرِة اللي عِند الأرْبعين حرامي. قرّر علي بابا ياخُد شْويِّةْ دهب ويِرْجع فيه عَ بَيْتو.

بعْد ما علي بابا رِجِع عَ البَيْت، خبّر لمرْتو اللي صار وقلّا عن الكنْز اللي لاقاه. خبّوا الدّهب وتّفقوا يِسْتعْمْلوه بِحذر كِرْمال يْحسّنوا حَياتُن. بسّ علي بابا كان عِنْدو خَيْ طمّاع إسْمو قاسِم، ولمّا عِرِف شو صار، كان بدّو ياخُد جِزْء مِن الكنْز لحالو.

راح قاسِم عَ المْغارة وسْتعْمل كِلْمةْ السّرّ كِرْمال يِفْتح المدْخل.

لمّا فات عَ المْغارة، ما قِدِر يْسيْطِر على طمعو، وأخد كمّية كْبيرة مِن الدّهب والكْنوز. بسّ لمّا جرّب يِضهر، نِسي كِلْمِةْ السّرّ ونْحبس بِالمْغارة.

هُوّ وقاسِم محْبوس جُوّا المْغارة، رِجِع الأربعين حرامي ولاقوه. قاصصوه وقتلوه لِأنّو جرّب يِسْرُق كِنْزُن. لمّا عِرِف علي بابا بِاللي صار لخيّو، زِعِل وخاف. قرّر ياخُد اِحْتِياطات كِرْمال يِحْمي عيلْتو مِن الأربعين حرامي اللي حَيْجرّبوا يِنْتِقْموا مِن دون شكّ.

بِنفس الوَقِت، كان عنْد علي بابا خِدّامِة ذكية ومُخْلِصة إسْما مُرْجانة. لمّا عِرْفِت خطر الحرامية، عِمْلِت خُطّة كِرْمال تِتْصرّف معُن. وبِمُساعْدِةْ علي بابا وإبنو، قِدِرت مُرْجانة تِقْضي على الأربعين حرامي وتِتْخلّص مِنُّن بِشكِل نِهائي.

بعْد ما قضيوا على الأربعين حرامي، ضلّ علي بابا وعيلْتو يِسْتعْمْلوا الكْنوز بْجِكْمة كِرْمال يِحسّنوا حَياتُن ويْساعْدوا الفُقرا والمِحْتاجين بْضيْعِتُن. تْجوّز إبن علي بابا مُرْجانة كنوْع مِن التّقْدير لشجاعِتا وذكاها، وعاشوا كِلُّن حَياةْ سعيدة ومُسْتقِرّة.

خلّصِت شهرزادْ قُصّةْ علي بابا والأَرْبعين حرامي، وكان المِلِك شهْرَيار مُتحمِّس إنّو يِسْمع قُصّة جْديدِة ومُلْهْمِة بِاللّيْلِة اللي بِعْدا.

## Questions

1. علي بابا شو كان بيشْتِغِل؟

2. كيف علي بابا كْتشف محل كنْز الأرْبعين حرامي؟

3. قاسِم شو عِمِل لمّا عِرِف مَوْضوع الكنْز؟

4. كيف مات قاسِم؟

5. مين هِيّ مُرْجانة وشو دَوْرا بِالْقُصّة؟

# Answers

1. علي بابا كان زلمي بسيط وفقير بيجمّع حطب بِالْغابة.

2. كْتشفو هُوّ وعم بيجمّع حطب وسِمِع صوْت حَوافِر على الأرْض ورْجال بيحْكوا بِصوْت عالي. وشافُن بيسْتعْمْلوا كِلِمْةْ السِّرّ كِرْمال يِفْتحوا المْغارة.

3. راح قاسِم عَ المْغارة وسْتعْمل كِلْمِةْ السِّرّ ليِفْتح الباب، وأخد كمّية كْبيرة مِن الدّهب والكْنوز.

4. مات قاسِم لمّا الأرْبعين حرامي رِجْعوا ولاقوه جُوّا المْغارة وقتلوه لِأنّو جرّب يِسْرق كنْزُن.

5. مُرْجانة كانِت خِدّامِةْ علي بابا الذّكية المُخْلِصة، ولِعْبِت دوْر مْهِمّ بِالتّخلُّص مِن الأرْبعين حرامي بِمُساعِدةْ علي بابا وإبْنو.

## Chapter 5: Ali Baba and the Forty Thieves

When Scheherazade finished the story of Aladdin and the Magic Lamp, King Shahryar was excited to hear more amazing stories full of adventures. That night, Scheherazade began to tell the story of Ali Baba and the Forty Thieves.

Ali Baba was a simple and poor man who lived in a remote village with his wife and son. One day, while he was gathering firewood in the forest, he heard the sound of hooves on the ground and the loud voices of men. He saw a man who appeared to be the leader of a group of forty thieves, and when they approached a huge rock, the leader said a secret word: "Open sesame!" and the rock opened to reveal a secret entrance to a huge cave filled with treasures and gold.

After the thieves left the cave, Ali Baba approached the huge rock and used the secret word to open the entrance. When he entered the cave, he was amazed by the enormous treasures that the forty thieves possessed. Ali Baba decided to take some gold and return home with it.

After his return home, Ali Baba explained to his wife what had happened and told her about the treasure he had discovered. They hid the gold and decided to use it cautiously to improve their lives. However, Ali Baba had a greedy brother named Qasim, and when he discovered what had happened, he wanted to take a portion of the treasure for himself.

Qasim went to the cave and used the secret word to open the entrance. When he entered the cave, he could not control his greed and collected a huge amount of gold and treasures. But when he tried to leave, he forgot the secret word and became trapped inside the cave.

While Qasim was trapped inside the cave, the forty thieves returned and found him. They punished him severely and killed him for attempting to steal their treasure. When Ali Baba learned of his brother's fate, he felt sadness and fear. He decided to take measures to protect his family from the forty thieves, who would undoubtedly seek revenge.

At the same time, Ali Baba had a smart and loyal servant named Morgiana. When she learned of the danger posed by the thieves, she devised a plan to get rid of them. With the help of Ali Baba and his son, Morgiana was able to eliminate the forty thieves and get rid of them for good.

After defeating the forty thieves, Ali Baba and his family continued to use the treasure wisely to improve their lives and help the poor and needy in their village. Ali Baba's son married Morgiana in honor of her bravery and intelligence, and they all lived a happy and stable life.

Scheherazade finished telling the story of Ali Baba and the Forty Thieves, and King Shahryar was eager to hear a new and inspiring story the following night.

Questions

1. What was Ali Baba's profession?
2. How did Ali Baba discover the location of the Forty Thieves' treasure?
3. What did Qasim do when he learned about the treasure?
4. How did Qasim die?
5. Who is Morgiana, and what was her role in the story?

Answers

1. Ali Baba was a simple and poor man who collected firewood in the forest.
2. Ali Baba discovered the location when he was collecting firewood and heard the sound of horses' hooves and the noise of men speaking loudly, and saw them using the secret word to open the entrance to the cave.
3. Kasim went to the cave and used the secret word to open the entrance, and collected a huge amount of gold and treasures.
4. Kasim died when the Forty Thieves returned and found him inside the cave, and killed him for attempting to steal their treasure.

5. Morgiana was Ali Baba's smart and loyal servant and played a crucial role in getting rid of the Forty Thieves with the help of Ali Baba and his son.

# الفَصْل السّادِس
## الفِلّاح الذّكي والجِنّي المُشاغِب

بِاللّيْلِة اللي بعْدا، بلّشِت شهْرزاد تِحْكي قُصّة جْديدِة لِلْمِلِك شهْرَيار عن فِلّاح ذكي وجِنّي مُشاغِب.

كان في فِلّاح فقير إسْمو يوسِف عايِش بِضيْعة صْغيرِة. يوسِف كان بْيِشْتِغِل كْتير كِرْمال يْأمِّن عَيْشو ويِقْدر يِطْعمي عيْلتو. بِيوْم مُشْمِس حِلو، قرّر يوسِف يْروح عَ الحقْلِة كِرْمال

يُقْطُف شُوَيّةْ فْواكِه وخُضرا يْبيعُن بِالسّوق. وهُوّعم بْيُحْفُر بِالأَرْض، خبط الفأس تبعو بِجرّة غريبة مدفونة تحْت الأرْض.

فتح يوسِف الجرّة ولاقى جُوّاتا جِنّي قديم مُشاغِب. قال الجِنّي لِيوسِف: "أنا محبوس بِالجرّة هَيْدي صِرْلي سْنين طويلة. شُكْراً لِأنّو ضهّرْتْني! بسّ لازِم حَذّرك، أنا جِنّي مُشاغِب وحجرِّب أضحك عليك. لح أعطيك تْلات أُمْنِيّات، بسّ لازِم تنْتِبِه وتِفكّر مْنيح قبِل ما تُطْلُب شي."

يوسِف كان زلمي حكيم وذكي وقرّر إنّو يِستعْمِل أُمْنِيّاتو بِحذر. أوّل شي طلبو إنّو يْكون غني لَيِقدر يْوَفّر حَياةْ أحسن لعيْلتو. الجِنّي عطاه دهب ومُجَوْهرات كْتير، وهوْل غيّروا حَياةْ يوسِف وعيْلتو لحَياةْ مِرتاحة.

بعديْن، طلب يوسِف مِن الجِنّي يْوَفّرلضيْعتو ماي نْضيفة كْتير للشُّرْب والرّيّ. حقّق الجِنّي الأمْنية هَيْدي وظهر نبْع جْديد بِالضيْعة بْتِطْلع مِنّو ماي نْضيفة ومُنْعِشة.

و بِالآخِر، طلب يوسِف مِن الجِنّي يَعْطي حِكْمِة وفِهِم أعْمق لَيْساعِد أَهِل قَرْيِتو ويِحْميُن مِن الخطر. وافق الجِنّي وعطى يوسِف الحِكْمة والفِهِم اللي طلبُن.

بِفضِل حِكِمْتو الجْديدِة، قِدِر يوسِف يْساعِد النّاس بِالضّيْعة ويْلاقي حْلول مُبتكرة لِلْمشاكِل والتّحدّيات اللي كانِت بِتْواجْهُن. مع مُرور الوَقِت، صار يوسِف شخْصية مُحترِمة ومْقدّرة بِضيْعْتو.

بسّ الجِنّي ما كان مبْسوط لِأنّو ما قِدِر يِخْدع يوسِف بِالأُمْنِيّات التّلاتِة. قرّر الجِنّي إنّو يْجرّب يِخْدع يوسِف بِطُرُق تانْية. بلّش الجِنّي يَعْمُل مشاكِل وفَوْضى بِالضّيْعة، مِتِل تدْمير المحاصيل وحرق البْيوت والمشاكِل بيْن الفِلّاحين.

سْتَعْمل يوسِف حِكْمْتو وفِهْمو كِرْمال يْصلّح الضّرر اللي الجِنّي تْسبّب في ويهدّي الأوْضاع المُتْوتّرة بيْن الفِلّاحين. ومع الوَقِت، بلّش الجِنّي يِفْهم إنّو مِش حَيِقْدر يِضحك على يوسِف وإنّو قِدِر يِرْبح على مكرو بِذكا وحِكِمْتو.

بِالنّهايِة، قرّر الجِنّي يِتْرُك يوسِف وضيْعتو بِسلام ويْروح يْنبِّش

على حدا تاني يِقْدر يِضْحك عليْه. وعلى الرّغْم مِن إنّو الجِنّي فلّ، بسّ يوسِف بِحِكِمْتو ضلّ يْساعِد الفِلّاحين ويْحسِّن حَياتُن.

بعْد ما المِلك شهْرَيار سِمع قُصّة الفِلّاح الذّكي والجِنّي المُشاغِب، صار مُتْحمِّس كِرْمال يِسمع قُصص تانْية حِلْوة ومُلْهِمة فِيا دُروس قيِّمة. وهيْك، نطر بِفارِغ الصّبِر بِدايِة القُصّة الجايِة اللي شهْرزاد حِتِحْكِيا.

## Questions

1. شو اللي لاقاه يوسِف لمّا فأسُو خبط بِجرّة غريبة مدْفونِة تحْت الأرْض؟

2. قدّيْش كان عدد الأُمْنيّات اللي الجِنّي عطاها لَيوسِف؟

3. كيف يوسِف شتعْمل الحِكْمة اللي الجِنّي عطاه ياها؟

4. شو عِمل الجِنّي لمّا ما قِدِر يِخْدع يوسِف بِالأُمْنيّات التّلاتِة؟

5. يوسِف شو عِمل كِرْمال يواجِهْ المشاكِل اللي سبّبا الجِنّي بِالضّيْعة؟

# Answers

1. لِقي يوسِف جِنّي قديم مُشاغِب محبوس جُوّا الجرّة.

2. الجِنّي عطى يوسِف تْلات أُمْنِيّات: إنّو يْصير غني، ويْجيب ماي نْضيفة كْتير لِضيْعْتو، ويَعْطي حِكْمة وفِهِم عميق. وشو هِنّ؟

3. سْتعْمل يوسِف الحِكْمة كِرمال يْساعِد الفِلّاحين بِحلّ مشاكِلُن ويْلاقي حْلول مُبتكرة لِلتّحدّيّات اللي كانوا عن بيواجْهوه.

4. قرّر الجِنّي إنّو يْجرِّب يِخْدع يوسِف بِطُرُق تانْية وصار يَعْمُل مشاكِل وفَوْضى بِالضّيْعة.

5. سْتعْمل يوسِف حِكْمتو وفِهْمو كِرمال يْصلِّح الأضرار اللي سبّبا الجِنّي ويْهدّي الوَضع المِتوَتِّر بيْن الفِلّاحين.

## Chapter 6: The Clever Farmer and the Mischievous Genie

On the following night, Scheherazade began telling another story to King Shahryar about a clever farmer and a mischievous genie.

There was a poor farmer named Youssef who lived in a small village. Youssef worked hard to provide for his family and make ends meet. One sunny day, he decided to go to the field to pick some fruits and vegetables to sell at the market. While plowing the land, his plow hit a strange jar buried in the ground.

Youssef opened the jar to find an old and mischievous genie inside. The genie said to Youssef, "I have been trapped in this jar for centuries. Thank you for freeing me! But I must warn you, I am a mischievous genie, and I will try to deceive you. I will grant you three wishes, but you must be careful and think carefully before you ask for anything."

Youssef was a wise and clever man and decided to use his wishes carefully. He first wished to be rich so that he could provide a better life for his family. The genie granted him a lot of gold and jewels that turned Youssef and his family's life into a luxurious one.

Then, Youssef asked the genie to provide his village with clean and abundant water for drinking and irrigation. The genie also granted this wish, and a new spring appeared in the village that flowed with clean and refreshing water.

Finally, Youssef asked the genie to grant him wisdom and deeper understanding to help his village people and protect them from danger. The genie agreed and gave Youssef the wisdom and understanding he asked for.

With his new wisdom, Youssef was able to help the villagers solve their problems and find innovative solutions to the challenges they faced. Over time, Youssef became a respected and appreciated figure in his village.

However, the genie was not happy that he could not deceive Youssef with his three wishes. He decided to try to deceive Youssef in other ways. The genie began causing problems and chaos in the village, such as destroying crops, setting fire to homes, and inciting fights among villagers.

Youssef used his wisdom and understanding to fix the damage caused by the genie and calm the tense situations among the villagers. Over time, the genie realized that he could not deceive Youssef and that he had been defeated by his intelligence and wisdom.

In the end, the genie decided to leave Youssef and his village in peace and go in search of another person he could deceive. Despite the genie's departure, Youssef's wisdom continued to help the villagers and improve their lives.

After hearing the story of the clever farmer and the mischievous genie, King Shahryar became eager to hear more wonderful and inspiring stories that carry valuable lessons. And so, he eagerly awaited the start of the next story that Scheherazade would tell.

Questions

1. What did Youssef find when his plow collided with a strange jar buried underground?
2. How many wishes did the genie grant Youssef, and what were those wishes?
3. How did Youssef use the wisdom that the genie gave him?
4. What did the genie do when he couldn't deceive Youssef with his three requests?
5. What did Youssef do to confront the problems caused by the genie in the village?

Answers

1. Youssef found an old and mischievous genie trapped inside the jar.
2. The genie granted Youssef three wishes: to become rich, to provide his village with pure and abundant

water, and to give him wisdom and deeper understanding.

3. Youssef used the wisdom to help the villagers solve their problems and find innovative solutions to the challenges they faced.

4. The genie decided to try to deceive Youssef in other ways and began to cause problems and chaos in the village.

5. Youssef used his wisdom and understanding to repair the damage caused by the genie and calm the tense situations among the villagers.

# الفَصْل السّابِع
# حرامي إسْكَنْدَرية ورَئيس الشُّرْطة

بِاللّيْلِة اللي بعْدا، بلّشِت شهرزاد تِحْكي قُصّةْ حرامي إسْكَنْدرية ورَئيس الشُّرْطة لِلْمَلِك شهْرَيار.

بِمدينِةْ إسْكَنْدرية العَريقة، كان في حرامي شاطِر وماكِر إسْمو ياسِر، كان بِسْرُق مصاري النّاس الأغْنِيا وما حدا كان بِقْدر يِلْقطو. كان ياسِر يُخطّط مُنيح لِكِلّ عَمليةْ سِرْقة، كان بِدْرُس

البْيوت ونشاط الضَّحايا اليَوْمي قبِل ما يْنفِّذ خُطَّتو.

بِيوْم مِن الإيّام، سرق ياسِر بيْت تاجِر غني. وِعِي التّاجِر الصُّبِح لِقي إنّو كِلّ مُمْتلكاتو الغالْية خْتِفِت وما إلا أثر. ضِغْري راح لِعِنْد رئيس الشُّرْطة، وهَيْدا كان زلمي حكيم وجدّي وإسْمو عبْد الرّحمن، وخبّرو على الحادِثِة. قال التّاجِر: "سرقوا كِلّ ثِروْتي! ما في غيْر حرامي إسْكنْدرية المشْهور اللي عِمِل هيْك."

تْحرقس رئيس الشُّرْطة عبْد الرّحمن مِن وَرا مهارات الحرامي العجيبِة، وقرّر يُوَقِّف جرايِم السِّرقة هَيْدي ويُلْقِط الحرامي بإيدو. بلّش عبْد الرّحمن يْحقِّق ويْجمِّع معْلومات عن السِّرْقات ويْنبِّش على تفاصيل تْساعْدو يِوْصل للْحرامي.

بِليْلِة مِن اللَّيالي، كْتشف عبْد الرّحمن إنّو في حرامي ناوي يِسرُق قصِر واحد مِن الأغْنِيا. قرّر عبْد الرّحمن إنّو يِتْرصَّدْلو. وبِنُصّ اللّيْل، شاف عبْد الرّحمن ياسِر فايِت عالقصِر وعم بْيِسْتعْمِل حبِل كِرمال يِعزِبِش على الحيْط.

لمّا فات ياسِر عَ القصر، لِقي عبْد الرّحْمن ناظرو. قال عبْد الرّحْمن بِصوْت هادي: "خلص يا ياسِر، مُغامراتك خِلْصِت، إنْتَ هلّق بيْن إيديْن رئيس الشُّرطة."

تْفاجأ ياسِر لمّا شاف عبْد الرّحْمن، بسّ ما سْتسْلم بِسُهولِة. قال ياسِر: "يمْكِن حظّك كان حِلو هالْمرّة، بسّ مِش حِتقْدر تِلْقط كِلّ الحرامية بِإسكنْدرية."

ردّ عبْد الرّحْمن بِثِقة: "يمْكِن، بسّ اليْوم حإقْدر ألْقط أشْهر وأذْكى واحد فِيُن."

قِدِر عبْد الرّحْمن يِلْقط ياسِر بعْد مُطارْدة قصيرِة بِقلْب القصِر. ياسِر نْكمش، ونْحكم عليْه بِالإدانة بِكِلّ جرايْمو. بِالْمحْكمِة، سأل القاضي ياسِر: "ليْش قرّرِت تْكون حرامي وتِسْرُق مِن النّاس بدل ما تْطلِّع رِزْقك بِطريقة شرْعية؟"

ردّ ياسِر: "كِنْت فقير وما كان عِنْدي مهارات وَلا تعْليم يخلّيني عيش بِكرامِة. أنا ما كِنْت بدّي ضُرّ حدا، بسّ الظُّروف خلّتْني أخْتار المصير هيْدا."

فِهِم عبْد الرّحْمن إنّو الظُّروف الصّعْبِة كانِت سبب رئيسي وَرا

اِخْتِيار ياسِر لِحَياةْ الجريمِة. قرّر عبْد الرّحْمن يْساعِد ياسِر يْغيّر حَياتو ويَعْطي فُرْصة لَيْبْقى شخْص أحْسن. بعْد ما ياسِر خلّص مُدّة عُقوبْتو، جبْلُو عبْد الرّحْمن فُرْصة إنّو يِشْتِغِل حارِس لِبيْت واحد مِن التُّجار الأغْنِيا.

خلّصِت شهْرزاد قُصّة حرامي إسْكنْدرية ورئيس الشُّرْطة. القُصّة عجبِت المِلِك شهْرَيار وكان بدّو يِسْمع قُصص تانْية مُلْهِمة ومُثيرة. بِالطّريقة هَيْدي، شهْرزاد خلّت المِلِك شهْرَيار بِنْطُر للّيْلِة اللي بعْدا لَيِسْمع قُصّة تانْية.

القُصّة هَيْدي علّمِت المِلِك شهْرَيار والنّاس اللي سِمْعوا إنّو الظُّروف الصّعْبِة مُمْكِن تِجْبُر بعْض النّاس إنّن يِتصرّفوا تصرُّفات غلط، بسّ بعْد في أمل إنّن يْغيّروا حَياتُن ويسْعوا لمُسْتقْبل أحْسن بِمُساعْدِة بعْضُن. فِهِم المِلِك إنّو العدِل والرّحْمِة لازِم يْكونوا مَوْجودين بِحِكْمو وإنّو لازِم يْكون مِسْتعِدّ يَعْطي فُرص تانْية للمُسْتضْعفين بِممْلكْتو.

## Questions

1. شو هُوّ إسْم الحرامي اللي كان عم يِسْرُق مصاري النّاس الأغْنِيا بِإسْكنْدرية؟

2. ياسِر شو كان يَعْمِل قبِل ما يْنفِّذ خُطط السّرْقة؟

3. مين رئيس الشُّرْطة اللي قرّر يْوَقِّف جرايِم السّرْقة تبع ياسِر؟

4. كيف عبْد الرّحْمن قِدِر يِلْقط ياسِر؟

5. كيف عبْد الرّحْمن ساعد ياسِر بعْد ما اِنْتهِت مُدَّة عُقوبْتو؟

## Answers

1. إسْم الحرامي هُوّ ياسِر.

2. كان ياسِر يْخطّط مْنيح لِكِلّ عملية سِرْقة، كِرْمال هيْك كان يِدْرُس البْيوت والنّشاط اليَوْمي للضّحايا قبِل ما يْنفِّذ خُطّتو.

3. عَبْد الرّحْمن هُوّ رئيس الشُّرْطة اللي قرّر يَعْمُل هيْك.

4. عَبْد الرّحْمن كْتشف إنّو الحرامي ناوي يِسْرُق قصِر واحد مِن الأغْنِيا، وتْرصّدْلو.

5. عَبْد الرّحْمن وَقرْلو فُرْصة إنّو يِشْتِغِل حارِس لبيْت واحد مِن التُّجار الأغْنِيا.

## Chapter 7: The Thief of Alexandria and the Police Chief

The next night, Scheherazade began to tell the story of the Alexandria Thief and the Chief of Police to King Shahryar.

In the ancient city of Alexandria, there was a skilled and cunning thief named Yaser who robbed the wealth of rich people without being caught. Yaser planned carefully for each theft, and he studied the houses and daily schedules of his victims before executing his plans.

One day, Yaser stole from the house of a wealthy merchant. The merchant woke up to find that all his valuable possessions had disappeared without a trace. Immediately, he went to the Chief of Police, a wise and strict man named Abdulrahman, to report the incident. The merchant said, "All my wealth has been stolen! This can only be the work of the notorious Thief of Alexandria."

The extraordinary abilities of the thief intrigued the Chief of Police, Abdulrahman, who decided to put an end to these thefts and capture the thief himself. Abdulrahman began investigating and gathering information about the thefts and searching for details that could help him reach the thief.

One night, Abdulrahman discovered that the thief was planning to steal the palace of a nobleman. Abdulrahman decided to wait for him in ambush. And at midnight,

Abdulrahman saw Yaser sneaking into the palace and using a rope to climb the wall.

When Yaser entered the palace, he found Abdulrahman waiting for him patiently. Abdulrahman said calmly, "Your adventures have come to an end, Yaser. You are now in the hands of the Chief of Police."

Yaser was surprised by the presence of Abdulrahman, but he did not surrender easily. He said, "Maybe you were lucky this time, but you won't be able to catch all the thieves in Alexandria."

Abdulrahman answered confidently, "It may be true, but today I will be able to catch the most famous and cunning of them."

Abdulrahman managed to catch Yaser after a short chase inside the palace. Yaser was arrested and convicted of all his crimes. In court, the judge asked Yaser, "Why did you decide to become a thief and steal from people instead of earning your living legally?"

Yaser answered, "I was poor and had no skills or education that could enable me to live with dignity. I didn't want to hurt anyone, but circumstances forced me to choose this fate."

Abdulrahman realized that harsh circumstances were the main reason behind Yaser's choice of a life of crime. He decided to help Yaser change his life and provide him with an opportunity to become a better person. After Yaser served his sentence, Abdulrahman provided him with a job opportunity as a guard in a a wealthy merchant's house.

Scheherazade finished telling the story of the Alexandria thief and the police chief. King Shahryar was impressed by this story and wanted to hear more inspiring and exciting stories. Thus, Scheherazade forced King Shahryar to wait until the next night to hear another story.

This story taught King Shahryar and the people who heard it that harsh circumstances could force some people to commit bad deeds, but there is still hope to redirect their lives and work towards a better future with the help of others. The king remembered that justice and mercy should prevail in his rule and that he should be prepared to provide second chances to the less fortunate in his kingdom.

Questions

1. What is the name of the thief who was stealing the wealth of rich people in Alexandria?
2. What was Yaser doing before carrying out his robbery plans?
3. Who is the police chief who decided to put an end to Yaser's robberies?
4. How did Abdulrahman manage to arrest Yaser?

5. How did Abdulrahman help Yaser after he served his sentence?

Answers

1. Yaser is the name of the thief.

2. Yaser was carefully planning each robbery, where he would study the houses and the daily schedules of his victims.

3. Abdulrahman is the police chief who made that decision.

4. Abdulrahman discovered that the thief planned to steal from the palace of a nobleman and waited for him in an ambush.

5. Abdulrahman provided him with a job opportunity as a guard in a a wealthy merchant's house.

# الفَصْل التّامِن
# العُصفور الأزْرق

بِاللّيْلة اللي بعْدا، بلّشِت شهْرزاد تِحْكي لِلْملِك شهْرَيار قُصَّةْ العصْفور الأزْرق.

بِبلد بْعيد كان في ملِك طيّب ومرْتو الملِكة. كان عنْدُن بِنت حِلْوة إسْما الأميرة ليْلى. مع إنّا كانِت حِلْوة ونبيلِة، بسّ ليْلى كانِت حزينِة لإنّا ما لاقِت حُبّ حَياتا. بِيوْم مِن الإيّام هيّ وعم

تِتْمشّى بْجْنيْنِةْ القِصِر، سِمْعِت عصْفورعم بيغنّي بِصوْت حِلو ولَوْنو أزْرق فاتِح، عصْفور ما حدا شاف مِتْلو مِن قبْل.

فكّرِت الأميرة ليْلى إنّو العصْفور الأزْرق هَيدا مُمْكِن يْكون مِفْتاح سعادِتا، فا قرّرِت إنّا تِنبّش عليْه. طلبِت مِن بيّا المِلِك يِعْلِن مُسابقة يُطْلُب فِيا مِن المُشارِكين إنُّن ينبشوا على العصْفور الأزْرق ويْلِقْطولا ياه. وافق المِلِك على الفِكْرة وأعْلن المُسابْقة لكلّ شباب المملكِة.

إجا عدد كْبير مِن الشّباب على القِصِر لَيشارْكوا بِالْمُسابْقة ويْنبّشوا على العصْفور الأزْرق. مِن بيْن المُشارِكين، كان في شبّ فقير إسْمو ياسين. ياسين كان بيحِبّ الأميرة ليْلى، وكان بدّو يْفرّحا بإنّو يْلاقي العصْفور الأزْرق. ما كان معو مصاري وَلا منْصِب يْخلّيه مُناسِب لِلأميرة، بسّ كان ذكي وشُجاع وعنْدو عزيمة.

بلّش ياسين رِحْلتو الطّويلة لَيْلاقي العصْفور الأزْرق. مرّت الإيّام والأسابيع والشّهور مِن دون فايْدة. وبِهَيْدي الرِّحْلِة، قابل ياسين ناس كْتير ساعدوه وعطيوه مَعْلومات جْديدِة عن مطْرح العصْفور الأزْرق.

بِالاَخِر، كْتشف ياسين إنّو العصْفور الأزرق عايِش بِجزيرِة بْعيدِة بِنُصّ البحْر. قرّر ياسين يْروح عَ الجزيرِة هَيْدي لَيْلقط العصْفور ويرْجع في لعِنْد الأميرة ليْلى. بعْد إيّام طويلة مِن التّعب والعَواصِف القويّة بِالبحْر، وِصِل ياسين عَ الجزيرِة البْعيدِة.

بلّش ياسين يِسْتكْشِف الجِزيرة وقابل صُعُبات ومخْلوقات غريبِة، بسّ ما سْتسْلم. بعْد بحِث صعِب وإصْرار، لِقي ياسين العصْفور الأزرق وقِدِر يِمْسكو. رِجِع ياسين، هُوّ وكْتير مبْسوط، بِالْعصْفور الأزْرق للْممْلكِة.

لمّا رِجِع ياسين وفرْجى العصْفور الأزرق للأميرة ليْلى، فِرْحوا النّاس كِلُّن ونْدهشوا. حْتفل المِلك بِعوْدِة ياسين وأعْلن إنّو ربِح المُسابقة. بسّ الأميرة ليْلى ما كانِت بدّا بسّ العصْفور الأزرق، كمان كانِت بدّا الشّب اللي راح لِاخِر الدّني لَيْفرّحا.

تْجوِّزِت الأميرة ليْلى ياسين، بعْد مُوافِقِةْ المِلك والملِكة. عاش ياسين والأميرة ليْلى حَياة سعِيدة ملْيانة حُبّ ورّفاهية. وعلّمِت القُصّة المِلك شهْرَيار والنّاس إنّو الإصْرار والشّجاعة

والحُبّ بْيِقْدروا يِرْبحوا على أيّ تحدّي ومُمْكِن يْوَصّلوا النّاس لِلسّعادة الحقيقية.

وهيْك، خِلِص الفصل التّامِن مِن حْكايات ألف ليْلِة وليْلِة. ما كان قدّام المِلِك شهرَيار غيْر إنّو يِنْطُر بِفارِغ الصّبِر لِلّيْلِة اللي جايِة لَيِستمْتِع بِقُصّة جْديدِة تْخبّرو ياها شهْرزاد.

بِاللّيْلِة اللي بعْدا، جْتمعوا المِلِك شهرَيار وشهْرزاد مرّة تانْيِة. وكان المِلِك مْحمّس كْتير إنّو يِسمع قُصص تانْيِة مُلْهِمة ومُثيرة. حسّ المِلِك شهرَيار إنّو الحكايات هيْدي غيّرِت حَياتو لِلأحْسن، وإنّا علّمِتو دُروس قيّمة عن العدِل والحِكْمة والحُبّ.

و على هيْدا الحال، ضلّت شهْرزاد تِحْكي قُصصا لِلمِلِك شهرَيار ليْلِة وَرا ليْلِة، بِمُحاوْلِة إنّا تِعلّمو وتِعلّم شعْبو دُروس تانْيِة مُهِمّة عن الحَياةْ والإنْسانية.

## Questions

١. الأميرة ليْلى شو كانِت حاسّة؟ وليْش؟

٢. شو طلِبِت الأميرة ليْلى مِن بيّا الملِك؟

٣. مين ياسين؟ وشو اللي خلّاه يِشْترِك بِالْمُسابْقة؟

٤. كيف عِرِف ياسين ويْن ساكِن العصْفور الأزْرق؟

٥. شو صار لمّا رِجِع ياسين بِالْعصْفور الأزْرق عَ المملكِة؟

# Answers

1. كانِت الأميرة ليْلى حاسّة بِالْحُزْن لِأنّو ما لاقِت حُبّ حَياتا.

2. طلِبت الأميرة ليْلى مِن بيّا الملِك إنّو يِعْلُن مُسابْقة يُطْلُب فِيا مِن المُشارْكين إنُّن يِنبشوا على العصْفور الأزْرق ويْجيبو للأميرة.

3. ياسين هُوّ شبّ فقير كان بيحِبّ الأميرة ليْلى وبدّو يِفرِّحا بِإنّو بِجيبْلا العصْفور الأزْرق.

4. عِرِف ياسين إنّو العصْفور الأزْرق كان عايِش بِجِزيرة بْعيدِة بِنُصّ البحر.

5. نْبسطوا النّاس ونْدهشوا لمّا رِجِع ياسين بِالْعصْفور الأزْرق، وحْتفل الملِك بِفوْزو بِالمُسابْقة، وتْجوِّزِت الأميرة ليْلى ياسين.

## Chapter 8: The Blue Bird

On the following night, Scheherazade began to tell King Shahryar the story of the Blue Bird.

In a faraway land, there was a kind king and his queen. They had a beautiful daughter named Princess Leila. Despite her beauty and nobility, Leila felt unhappy because she had not yet found the love of her life. One day, while walking in the palace garden, she heard the singing of a beautiful bird with bright blue feathers. No one had ever seen a bird like this before.

Princess Leila thought that the Blue Bird might be the key to her happiness, so she decided to search for it. She asked her father, the king, to announce a contest in which all the participants must search for the Blue Bird and bring it to her. The king agreed to the idea and announced the contest to all the young men in the kingdom.

Many young men came to the palace to participate in the contest and search for the Blue Bird. Among them was a poor young man named Yassin. Yassin was in love with Princess Leila and wanted to make her happy by finding the Blue Bird. He did not have wealth or a position that would be suitable for the princess, but he had intelligence, bravery, and determination.

Yassin began his long journey to search for the Blue Bird. Days, weeks, and months passed without any success. On this journey, he faced many challenges and dangers, but he did not give up. During his journey, Yassin met many people who helped him and provided him with new information about the whereabouts of the Blue Bird.

In the end, Yassin discovered that the Blue Bird lived on a remote island in the middle of the sea. He decided to sail to this island to find the bird and bring it back to Princess Leila. After many days of suffering and violent storms at sea, Yassin arrived at the remote island.

Yassin explored the island and faced many obstacles and strange creatures, but he did not give up. After a long search and perseverance, Yassin found the Blue Bird and managed to catch it. With great joy, Yassin returned to the kingdom with the Blue Bird.

When Yassin returned and showed the Blue Bird to Princess Leila, everyone's hearts filled with happiness and amazement. The king celebrated Yassin's return and announced his victory in the contest. But Princess Leila did not only want the Blue Bird; she also wanted the young man who went to the ends of the earth to make her happy.

Princess Leila married Yassin with the approval of the king and queen. Yassin and Princess Leila lived a happy life filled with love and prosperity. The story taught King Shahryar and the people that determination, bravery, and love could overcome any challenge and lead to true happiness.

And so, the eighth chapter of the Tales of One Thousand and One Nights came to an end. King Shahryar could only wait eagerly for the next night to hear another inspiring and exciting story from Scheherazade.

On the following night, King Shahryar and Scheherazade gathered again, where the king was eager to hear more inspiring and exciting stories. King Shahryar felt that these stories had changed his life for the better and taught him valuable lessons about justice, wisdom, and love.

And so, Scheherazade continued to tell her stories to King Shahryar night after night, trying to teach him and his people more important lessons about life and humanity.

Questions

1. What was Princess Leila feeling and why?
2. What did Princess Leila ask her father, the king, for?
3. Who is Yasin, and what made him participate in the competition?
4. Where did Yasin learn that the blue bird lived?
5. What happened when Yasin returned with the blue bird to the kingdom?

6. How did people's lives improve in the kingdom after the princess's return?

## Answers

1. Princess Leila was feeling sad because she had not found the love of her life.

2. Princess Leila asked her father, the king, to announce a competition to search for and bring her the blue bird.

3. Yasin is a poor young man who is in love with Princess Leila and wants to make her happy by bringing her the blue bird.

4. Yasin learned that the blue bird lived on a remote island in the middle of the sea.

5. Everyone's hearts were filled with joy and amazement when Yasin returned with the blue bird. The king celebrated his victory in the competition, and Princess Leila married Yasin.

# الفَصْل التّاسِع
# البِنْت والسّاحْرة

بِاللّيْلِة اللي بعْدا، سْتعدّ المِلك شهْرَيار لَيِسْمع قُصّة جْديدِة مِن شهْرزاد. بلّشِت شهْرزاد تِحْكي حِكاية البِنْت والسّاحْرة.

بِيوْم مِن الإيّام، بِضيْعة بْعيدِة، كان في بِنْت صبِيّة إسْما لينا. كانِت لينا ساكْنة مع إمّا المريضة وخيّا الصّغير. كانوا فُقرا وبِيكافْحوا لأنْجأ يْأَمْنوا اِحْتِياجاتُن اليَوْمية. بِيوْم مِن الإيّام،

راحِت لينا عَ الْغابِة لِتِجْمع فُطُر وتوت لعيْلِتا. هيّ وعم تِتمشّى بِالْغابة، سِمْعِت صوْت ضْعيف عم بيعيِّطْلا.

مِشْيِت لينا وَرا الصّوْت لِحدّ ما لاقِت سِتّ خِتْيارة. كانِت السِّتّ كْتير ضْعيفِة، وكانِت بِتْجرِّب تدفّي حالا مِن البرِد. لمّا لينا شافِت حالِتا الصّعْبِة، قرّرِت تْساعِدا. فا أخدِت السِّتّ لبيْتا وقدِّمِتْلا أكِل ومطرح تْنام فيه. على الرّغْم مِن الفُقِر اللي كانِت عايْشِة فيه عيِلْتا، بسّ لينا كانِت كريمِة وحنونِة.

بعْد ما السِّتّ ردَّت قُوِّتا، قالِت لِلينا إنّا بِالْحقيقة ساحْرة قَويّة. وإمْتِنانًا لِلينا ولطيبِةْ قلْبا وكرما، عرضِت السّاحْرة على لينا تْحقّقْلا تْلات أُمْنِيّات. فكّرِت لينا شْوَيّ وقرّرِت تُطلُب الشّفا لإمّا، وتْحسَّن حَياةْ خيّا، والثّرْوَة لتْوَفِّر حَياةْ أحْسن لعيْلِتا.

وافِقِت السّاحْرة على تِحْقيق أُمْنِيّات لينا، وحسّنِت حَياةْ عيِلْتا. رِجْعِت الصّحّة والنّشاط لإمّ لينا، وخيّا قِدِر يْروح عَ المدْرسِة ويِتْعلّم. وبِفضْل الثّرْوِة قِدِرت عيْلِة لينا تِبْني بيْت جْديد وتْوَفِّر حَياةْ مُريحة لِأفْرادا.

مرّت السنين، وتحسّنِت أحْوال العيْلِة بِفضْل المُساعْدة السّحْرية. كِبرِت لينا وصارِت بِنْت حِلْوة وذكية وشُجاعة. كانِت دايْماً تِتْذكّر عطْف السّاحْرة علَيا وعلى عيْلِتا، وكِرْمال هيْك قرّرِت تْساعِد النّاس بِضيْعِتا. صارِت معْروفة بِحِكْمِتا ورحْمِتا، لِأنّو كانِت بِتْقدّم المشورة والمُساعْدِة لِجيرانا.

بِيوْم مِن الإيّام، قرّب مِن لينا شبّ غريب وطلب مُساعْدِتا. كانِت الضيْعة مُهدّدة مِن مجموعِةْ حرامية بدّن يِسرْقوا أمْلاك النّاس ويِرعْبووُن. سْتعانِت لينا بِذكاها وشجاعِتا لتْنظّم الفِلّاحين وتِقاوِم الحراميّة. بعْد المُواجهة الشّرْسة، قِدْروا يِرْبحوا الحراميّة ويحْموا الضيْعة.

بِفضْل شجاعِتا وحِكْمِتا، صارِت لينا زعيمِة إلا اِحْتِراما بِالضّيْعة. تْجوّزِت الشبّ اللي طلب مُساعْدِتا، وعِمْلوا عيْلِة جْديدِة مع بعْض. عاشِت لينا حَياةْ سعيدِة ومُسْتقرِّة، وضلَّت تْساعِد الضيْعة بِحِكْمِتا وقُوَّتا. رِبْحِت حُبّ واِحْتِرام كِلّ النّاس اللي بِالضّيْعة لِكِلّ التّضْحِيّات والمُساعْدات اللي قدّمِتا.

خلّصِت شهْرزاد قُصّةْ البِنْت والسّاحْرة الخِتْيارة، وكان المِلِك شهْرَيار عم يِسْمع القُصّة وهُوّ مُتشوّق. ورغْم إنّا كانِت قُصّة مُخْتلِفة عن القُصص اللي قبْلا، بسّ هُوّ سْتمْتع فِيا وكان مُتحمِّس لَيِسْمع القُصّة اللي بعْدا.

## Questions

1. شو اللي كانِت لينا عم تِعْمْلُو بِالْغابِة قبِل ما تْقابِل السِّتّ الخِتْيارة؟

2. كيف لينا ساعْدِت السِّتّ الخِتْيارة؟

3. شو كشِفِت عن حالا السِّتّ الخِتْيارة بعْد ما ردَّت قُوَّتا؟

4. شو التْلات أُمْنِيّات اللي طلِبِتُن لينا مِن السّاحْرة؟

5. كيف لينا أنْقِذِت ضيْعِتا مِن مُجْموعِةْ الحرامية؟

## Answers

1. كانِت لينا عم بِتْجمّع فُطُر والتّوت بِالْغابِة لِلْعيْلِتا.

2. أخدِت لينا السِّتّ الخِتْيارة لبَيْتا وقدّمِتْلا أكِل ومطرح تْنام فيه.

3. كشِفِت السِّتّ الخِتْيارة إنّا بِالْحقيقة ساحْرة قَوية.

4. إنّو إمّا تْصُحّ، وتحْسين حَياةْ خيّا، والثَّرْوِة كِرْمال تْوَفِّر حَياةْ أحْسن لعيْلِتا.

5. سْتعانِت لينا بِذكاها وشجاعِتا لتْنظِّم الفِلّاحين وتْواجِهْ الحرامية. وبعْد المُواجْهة الشِّرْسِة، قِدروا يِرْبحوا الحرامية ويحْموا الضيْعة.

## Chapter 9: The Girl and the Magical Old Woman

On the next night, King Shahryar prepared himself to listen to a new story from Scheherazade. Scheherazade began to narrate the story of the girl and the sorceress.

Once upon a time, in a faraway village, there was a young girl named Lena. Lena lived with her sick mother and younger brother. They were poor and struggled to make ends meet. One day, Lena went to the forest to gather mushrooms and berries for her family. While wandering in the forest, she heard a weak voice calling her.

Lena followed the voice until she reached an old woman. The old woman appeared frail and weak, and she was trying to shelter from the cold. When Lena saw her miserable condition, she decided to help her. The girl took the old woman to her house, where she provided her with food and shelter. Despite the poverty that her family lived in, Lena was kind and compassionate.

After the old woman regained her strength, she revealed to Lena that she was actually a powerful sorceress. In gratitude for Lena's kindness and generosity, the sorceress offered Lena three wishes. Lena thought about it and decided to ask for her mother's healing, to improve her brother's life, and wealth to provide a better life for her family.

The sorceress agreed to fulfill Lena's wishes and transformed the family's life for the better. Lena's mother became healthy and active again, and her brother was able to go to school and learn. Thanks to the wealth they acquired, Lena's family was able to build a new house and provide a comfortable life for themselves.

Years passed, and the family flourished thanks to the magical help. Lena grew up to become a beautiful, intelligent, and brave girl. She always remembered the sorceress's kindness to her and her family and therefore decided to help others in her village. She became known for her wisdom and compassion, offering advice and assistance to her neighbors.

One day, a strange young man approached Lena and asked for her help. The village was threatened by a group of thieves who sought to steal people's possessions and intimidate them. Lena used her intelligence and courage to organize the villagers and confront the thieves. After a fierce confrontation, they managed to defeat the thieves and secure the village.

Thanks to her courage and wisdom, Lena became a respected leader in her village. She married the young man who asked for her help, and they started a new family together. Lena lived a happy and stable life and continued to help the village with her wisdom and strength. She won the love and respect of all the villagers for her sacrifices and assistance.

Scheherazade finished narrating the story of the girl and the sorceress, and King Shahryar eagerly listened to the story. Although it was a different story from the previous ones, he enjoyed it and was eager to hear the next story.

Questions

1. What was Lena doing in the forest before meeting the old woman?
2. How did Lena help the old woman?
3. What did the old woman reveal about herself after regaining her strength?
4. What were the three wishes that Lena asked the sorceress for?
5. How did Lena rescue her village from the group of thieves?

Answers

1. Lena was collecting mushrooms and berries for her family in the forest.
2. Lena took he old woman to her home and provided her with food and shelter.
3. The old woman revealed that she was actually a powerful sorceress.

4. To heal her mother, improve her brother's life, and gain wealth to provide a better life for her family.

5. Lena relied on her intelligence and bravery to organize the villagers and confront the thieves, and after a fierce confrontation, they were able to defeat the thieves and secure the village.

# الفصْل العاشِر
## الأمير والتِّنين

بِاللّيْلِة اللي بعْدا، بلّشِت شهْرزاد تِحْكي حِكايِةْ الأمير والتِّنين لِلْملِك شهْرَيار.

بِممْلكِة بْعيدِة، كان في أمير شبّ وشُجاع إسْمو رامي. المملكِة كانِت بِتْعاني مِن هجمات مُتْكرِّرة مِن تِنين عِمْلاق عايِش بِجبل قريب. التِّنين كان يُهاجِم القُرى ويْخْطف

الشّباب والبنات لَياكِلُن. النّاس كانوا عايْشين بِخوْف كِلّ الوَقِت وما كانوا بِتْجرّؤوا يْواجْهوا التّنين العِمْلاق.

بِيوْم مِن الإيّام، قابل الأمير رامي زلمي مِن ضيْعة مِن الضّيع المنْكوبِة. قلّو الزّلمي: "يا أميرْنا، التّنين خطف بِنْتي الصّغيرِة، وصِرْنا عايْشين بِخوْف مِش قادْرين نِتْحمّلو. بِتْرجّاك تْخلِّصْنا مِن الوَحْش المُرْعِب هَيْدا."

قرّر الأمير رامي إنّو يْواجِهْ التّنين ويْخلِّص شعْبو مِن هَيْدا الكائِن المُرْعِب. سلّح حالو بِأحْسن الأسْلِحة والدُّروع وبلّش رِحْلتو لجبل التّنين. وضمْن رِحْلتو، قابل حكيم عَ جوز عطاه سْلاح سِحْري بْيِقْدر يِقْتُل في التّنين. قلّو الحكيم: "سْتعْمِل السّلاح السِّحْري هَيْدا بِحذر، هَيْدا الشّي الوَحيد اللي مُمْكِن يِقْتُل التّنين العِمْلاق."

وِصِل الأمير رامي لجبل التّنين ولِقي الوَحْش الكِبير نايِم. قرّر يُنْظر لَيوعى التّنين كِرْمال يْواجْهو بِشجاعة. لمّا وِعي التّنين، عيّط الأمير رامي وقلّو: "يا تِنين يا شِرّير، أنا حأُقْضي عليْك اليوْم وحخلِّص شعْبي مِن هُجوماتك الوَحْشية!"

ستعدّ لِمُواجْهِةْ التّنين، وسْتعْمِل السِّلاح السّحْري اللي الحكيم الخِتْيار عطى ياه. بلّشِت المعْركة بيْن الأمير رامي والتّنين العِمْلاق. كان التّنين عم بيرفرف بِجناحو ويْطلّع النّار مِن تِمّو بِاتِّجاه الأمير، وبِنفْس الوقْت كان رامي بيْتجنّبو بِمهارة وبيِسْتعْمِل سِلاحو السّحْري كِرْمال يْوَجّهْ لِلتّنين ضرْبات قَوية. سْتمرّت المعْركة لِساعات طَويلة، وكان الأمير رامي عم يِفْقُد قُوّتو شْوَيّ بْشْوَيّ.

بِلحْظة حاسِمة، سْتعان رامي بِكِلّ شجاعْتو وبِالقُوّة اللي ضلّت عِنْدو، وقِدِر يْوَجّهْ ضرْبة قاضْية لِلتّنين بِسْلاحو السّحْري. وقِع التّنين على الأرْض ومات، وهيْك أنْقذ الأمير رامي شعْبو مِن الوحْش المُرْعِب.

رِجِع الأمير رامي لِلْممْلِكة، وكان النّاس نظرينو كِرْمال يِحْتِفْلوا بِبْطولْتو. تْجمّعوا بْساحات المدينة وعِمْلوا مهْرجان كْبير كِرْمال يِحْتِفْلوا بِالأمير الشُّجاع. تْجوّز رامي أجْمل بِنْت بِالْممْلِكة وورِثْت العِرْش لمّا مات بيّو المِلِك.

حكم رامي الممْلِكة بِحِكْمة وعِدِل، وصار معْروف بِشجاعْتو وتضْحِيّاتو كِرْمال شعْبو. عاشِت الممْلِكة بِسلام ورخاء تِحِت

حِكْمو العادِل ونْتِهت مُعاناتُن مِن هجمات التِّنين أَوْ أيّ خطر تاني. وهَيْدي كانِت حِكايةْ الأمير رامي والتِّنين العِمْلاق اللي حكِتا شهْرزاد لِلْمِلِك شهْرَيار.

بَعْد ما سِمع المِلِك شهْرَيار حِكايةْ الأمير رامي والتِّنين، أبْدى إعْجاب كْبير بِشجاعِةْ الأمير وحِكِمْتو بِحُكْم المَمْلِكة.  وكان بْيِسْأل حالو، يا ترى، شو بيصير إذا بْيِقْدِر يِتْعلّم مِن تجارُب الأمير رامي ويْطبّقا بِممْلكْتو. فكّر المِلِك بِعُمق بِالْقُصص اللي سِمِعا مِن شهْرزاد، وبلّش يْشوف حالو بِمنْظور جْديد.

قرّر المِلِك شهْرَيار إنّو ما يِقْتُل شهْرزاد، مِش بسّ كِرْمال يِسمع حِكاياتا كِلّ لَيْلة، بسّ كمان لِأنّو الحِكايات تبعا كان إلا تأْثير كْبير على شخْصِيّتو وغيّرِتو لِلْأحْسن. صار مِلِك عادِل أكْتر، وألْطف، بِفِضْل الحِكايات هَيْدي اللي ألْهِمتو وعلّمتو قيمِةْ الرّحْمِة والإنْصاف.

بِالإيّام اللي بَعْدا، صار المِلِك شهْرَيار أكْتر عدْل ورحْمة بِحُكْمو. صار يِسْمع بِاهْتِمام لِشكاوى شعْبو، ونْشغل بِتصْليح الظُّلِم

وتحْسين حَياةْ النّاس. تْحوّلِت المملكِة لِمكان أحْسن للحَياةْ تحِت حُكْم الملِك شهْرَيار العادِل.

عاش الملِك شهْرَيار وشهْرزاد سَوا بِسعادِة ورخاء لسْنين طَويلِة. وضلَّت شهْرزاد تِحْكي الِحْكايات لِجوْزا الملِك شهْرَيار كِلّ ليْلِة، وكانِت الحْكايات هَيْدي سِرّ سعادِتُن وسعادِةْ ممْلكِتُن. وهيْك نْتِهت حِكايةْ شهْرزاد والملِك شهْرَيار اللي غيّرِت مصير ممْلكِة بحالا.

## Questions

1. شو كانِت المَمْلِكِة بِتْعاني مِنّو بِسبب التِّنين العِمْلاق؟

2. شو قرّر الأمير رامي يِعْمْلو لمّا سِمِع عن مُعاناةْ النّاس مِن التِّنين؟

3. مِن ويْن الأمير رامي جاب السْلاح السَّحْري؟

4. كيف الأمير رامي قِدِر يِقْتُل التِّنين؟

5. كيف النّاس اِحْتفلوا بعْد هزيمةْ التِّنين؟

6. شو اللي سألو المَلِك شهْرَيار لحالو بعْد ما سِمِع قُصّةْ الأمير رامي والتِّنين؟

7. كيف اِتْأثّر المَلِك شهْرَيار بِقُصص شهْرزاد؟

8. كيف تْغيِّرِت المَمْلِكِة تحْت حُكْم المَلِك شهْرَيار؟

9. كيف أثّرِت قُصص شهْرزاد على حَياةْ المَلِك شهْرَيار وشهْرزاد مع بعْض؟

10. كيف نْتِهِت حِكايِةْ شهْرزاد والمَلِك شهْرَيار؟

11. إزّاي اِنْتِهت حِكايِةْ شهْرزاد و الملِك شهْرَيار؟

## Answers

1. كانِت المملِكة بِتْعاني مِن هجمات مُتْكرِّرة للتِّنين العِمْلاق اللي كان بيهاجِم القُرى ويِخْطف الشّباب والبنات كِرْمال ياكلُن.

2. قرّر الأمير رامي يُواجِهْ التِّنين ويِنْقِذ شعْبو مِن الوَحْش المُرْعِب هَيْدا.

3. الأمير رامي جاب السْلاح السّحْري مِن حكيم خِتْيار قابلو بِرِحْلِتو لِجبل التِّنين.

4. قِدِر الأمير رامي يِقْتُل التِّنين بِاسْتِعْمال السْلاح السّحْري اللي عطاه ياه الحكيم الخِتْيار، ووَجّه في ضرْبِة قاضِية للتِّنين.

5. النّاس حْتفلوا بعْد هزيمِةْ التِّنين بِإنُّن تْجمّعوا بِساحات المدينة وعِمْلوا مهْرجان كْبير لِيِحْتِفْلوا بِالأمير الشُّجاع رامي.

6. المَلِك شهْرَيار سأل حالو يا ترى، شو بيصير لَوْ قِدِر يِتْعلّم مِن تجارُب الأمير رامي ويطبِّقا بِممْلكْتو.

7. تأثَّر المَلِك شهْرَيار بِشكِل عميق بِقُصص شهْرزاد اللي ألْهمِتو وعلّمِتو قيمة الرّحْمة والإنْصاف، وصار مِلِك أكْتر عادِل أكْتر، وألْطف.

8. تْحوَّلت المملِكة لمكان أفْضل للْحَياةْ تحِت حُكْم المَلِك شهْرَيار العادِل، لإنّو صار بْيِسْمع بِاهْتِمام لشكاوى شعْبو ونْشغل بِتصْليح الظُّلِم وتحْسين حَياةْ النّاس.

9. عاش المَلِك شهْرَيار وشهْرزاد مع بعْض بِسعادِة وازْدِهار لسْنين طويِلة، وضلِّت شهْرزاد تِحْكي الحْكايات لجَوْزا المَلِك شهْرَيار كِلّ لَيْلِة، وكانِت القُصص هَيْدي سِرّ سعادِتُن وسعادِة مملِكِتُن.

10. نْتِهِت حِكايِةْ شهْرزاد والمَلِك شهْرَيار بِتغْيير مصير ممْلِكِة كِلّا، وعاشوا مع بعْض بِسعادِة وازْدِهار لسْنين طويِلة، ضلّت شهْرزاد تِحْكي القُصص لجوْزا المَلِك شهْرَيار كِلّ لَيْلِة، وساهمِت القُصص هَيْدي

بِتحْسين علاقِتُن وعِمْلِت تِغْييرات إيجابية على مُسْتَوى المَمْلِكِة كِلّا.

## Chapter 10: The Prince and the Dragon

On the next night, Scheherazade began to tell the story of the prince and the dragon to King Shahryar.

In a faraway kingdom, there was a young and brave prince named Rami. The kingdom suffered from frequent attacks by a huge dragon that lived in a nearby mountain. The dragon would attack the villages and kidnap young boys and girls to eat them. The people lived in constant fear and did not dare to confront the giant dragon.

One day, Prince Rami met a man from one of the devastated villages. The man said to him, "Oh, our prince, the dragon has kidnapped my little daughter, and we live in unbearable fear. I beg you to save us from this terrifying monster."

Prince Rami decided to face the dragon and save his people from this terrifying creature. He prepared himself with the best weapons and armor and set out on his journey to the dragon's mountain. During his journey, he met a wise old man who gave him a magic weapon that could defeat the dragon. The wise man said to the prince, "Use this magic weapon carefully, for it is the only one that can defeat the giant dragon."

Prince Rami reached the dragon's mountain and found the huge monster sleeping. He decided to wait until the dragon woke up to face him bravely. When the dragon woke up,

Prince Rami shouted, "Oh, evil dragon, today I will kill you and save my people from your brutal attacks!"

He prepared to face the dragon and used the magic weapon given to him by the wise old man. The battle began between Prince Rami and the huge dragon. The dragon flapped its wings and breathed fire at the prince while Rami dodged skillfully and used his magic weapon to strike hard blows at the dragon. The battle continued for hours, and Prince Rami was slowly losing his energy.

In a decisive moment, Rami summoned all his courage and remaining strength and managed to deliver a fatal blow to the dragon using his magic weapon. The dragon fell to the ground and breathed its last breath, and thus, Prince Rami saved his people from the terrifying monster.

Prince Rami returned to the kingdom, where people awaited him eagerly to celebrate his bravery. They gathered in the city squares and held a big festival in honor of the brave prince. Rami married one of the most beautiful girls in the kingdom and inherited the throne when his father, the king, died.

Prince Rami ruled the kingdom wisely and fairly and became known for his courage and sacrifices for his people. The kingdom lived in peace and prosperity under his fair rule and did not suffer any more dragon attacks or other risks. This was the story of Prince Rami and the huge dragon told by Scheherazade to King Shahryar.

After hearing the story of Prince Rami and the dragon, King Shahryar expressed his deep admiration for the prince's bravery and wisdom in ruling his kingdom. He wondered what it would be like if he could learn from Prince Rami's experiences and apply them to his own kingdom. King Shahryar reflected on the stories he had heard from Scheherazade and began to see himself in a new light.

King Shahryar decided not to kill Scheherazade not only because he looked forward to hearing her stories every night, but also because her stories had a profound effect on his personality and had changed him for the better. He became a more just and kind king thanks to those stories that inspired him and taught him the value of mercy and fairness.

In the following days, King Shahryar became more just and merciful in his rule. He listened carefully to his people's complaints and worked hard to correct the injustice and improve people's lives. The kingdom turned into a better place to live under King Shahryar's fair rule.

King Shahryar and Scheherazade lived together in happiness and prosperity for many years. Scheherazade continued to tell stories to her husband, King Shahryar, every night, and those stories were the secret to their happiness and the happiness of their kingdom. And thus ended the story of Scheherazade and King Shahryar, which changed the fate of the entire kingdom.

Questions

1. What was the kingdom suffering from because of the giant dragon?
2. What did Prince Rami decide when he heard about the people's suffering from the dragon?
3. Where did Prince Rami get the magical weapon from?
4. How did Prince Rami manage to defeat the dragon?
5. How did the people celebrate after defeating the dragon?
6. What did King Shahryar wonder about after hearing the story of Prince Rami and the dragon?
7. How was King Shahryar affected by the stories of Scheherazade?
8. How did the kingdom change under King Shahryar's rule?
9. How did the stories of Scheherazade affect the lives of King Shahryar and Scheherazade together?
10. How did the story of Scheherazade and King Shahryar end?

Answers

1. The kingdom was suffering from frequent attacks by the giant dragon that would attack villages and kidnap young boys and girls to eat them.

2. Prince Rami decided to confront the dragon and save his people from this terrifying monster.

3. Prince Rami obtained the magical weapon from a wise old man he met during his journey to the dragon mountain.

4. Prince Rami managed to defeat the dragon by using the magical weapon given to him by the wise old man and delivering a fatal blow to the dragon.

5. The people celebrated after defeating the dragon by gathering in the city squares and holding a big festival to honor the brave Prince Rami.

6. King Shahryar wondered how it would be if he could learn from Prince Rami's experiences and apply them in his own kingdom.

7. King Shahryar was deeply influenced by the stories of Scheherazade, which inspired him and taught him the value of mercy and justice, and he became a more just and kind king.

8. The kingdom became a better place to live under the rule of the just King Shahryar, who listened carefully

to the complaints of his people and worked hard to correct injustices and improve their lives.

9. King Shahryar and Scheherazade lived together in happiness and prosperity for many years, with Scheherazade continuing to tell stories to her husband every night, and those stories were the secret of their happiness and the happiness of their kingdom.

10. The story of Scheherazade and King Shahryar ended with the change of the fate of the entire kingdom and making them live together in happiness and prosperity for many years, with Scheherazade continuing to tell stories to her husband every night, and these stories helped to strengthen their bond and bring about positive changes throughout the kingdom.

# lingualism

Visit our website for information on current and upcoming titles and free language learning resources.

# www.lingualism.com

www.ingramcontent.com/pod-product-compliance
Lightning Source LLC
Chambersburg PA
CBHW070151080526
44586CB00015B/1936